A Second Paradise

[1.] (DETAIL) A RAJPUT RULER SUBMITS TO EMPEROR AKBAR. MUGHAL, CA. 1590.

A Second Paradise

INDIAN COURTLY LIFE 1590-1947

With Illustrations by Bannu

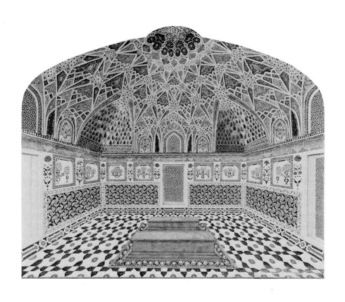

Introduction by Stuart Cary Welch
Text by Naveen Patnaik

Doubleday & Company, Inc. ● Garden City, New York

1985

Author's Note

To my sister, Gita Mehta, my deepest gratitude for her encouragement and guidance.
To Rajmata Gayatri Devi of Jaipur, Princess Sita of Kapurthala, and Begum Mehtab Zamani Ali
Khan of Rampur, my thanks for the hours they generously spent sharing
their knowledge of the subject and their memories.
I am grateful to Maharaja Gaj Singh of Jodhpur for making available to me
his collection of photographs and archival material.
My thanks to Rani Naina Devi for elucidating many aspects of Indian music, dance, and poetry.
Special thanks are due to Martand Singh, Mahijit Singh Jhala,
and Malvika Singh for their valuable assistance in my research.
Finally, I would like to thank Jacqueline Kennedy Onassis, who inspired this book
and whose advice and constant support made it possible.

Library of Congress Cataloging in Publication Data

Patnaik, Naveen.   A second paradise.   Bibliography: p. 189
1. India—Court and courtiers—Pictorial works.   I. Bannu.   II. Title.   DS423.P425 1985   954.03
ISBN 0-385-19992-9 LIBRARY OF CONGRESS CATALOG CARD NUMBER 84–25909
TEXT COPYRIGHT © 1985 BY NAVEEN PATNAIK   ILLUSTRATIONS COPYRIGHT © 1985 BY VED PAL SHARMA
INTRODUCTION COPYRIGHT © 1985 BY STUART CARY WELCH

DESIGNED BY MICHAEL FLANAGAN

Editor's Note

So many people helped to make this book possible that I find it difficult to adequately express my appreciation. Foremost, deepest thanks are due to Pupul Jayakar, Chairman of the Festival of India U.S.A. 1985, without whose permission and kindness this book would not have been possible. And to Martand Singh, Indian National Trust for Art and Cultural Heritage, whose sensibility and unflagging zeal consistently helped us on our way. For guiding us through their collections and for assisting in many ways, my appreciation to the director and staff of these museums and institutions: National Museum, Delhi; Sawai Man Singh II Museum, the City Palace, Jaipur; Mehrangarh Museum, Jodhpur Fort, Jodhpur; State Museum, Lucknow; Picture Gallery, Lucknow; Talukedar's Baradari, Kaiserbagh, Lucknow; La Martinière, Lucknow; Salar Jung Museum, Hyderabad; Raja Deen Dayal Photographic Studio, Hyderabad; Khuda Baksh Oriental Public Library, Patna; Handicrafts and Handlooms Export Corporation.

For their warm and generous hospitality, for showing us their family costumes and the settings in which they were worn, my gratitude to the following people. In Hyderabad: the Nizam of Hyderabad; Princess Esin Jah of Hyderabad; Nahid, Begum Sahida; Nawab Ahmed Yar Jung; Begum Basheer Yar Jung; Mrs. Laxmi Devi Raj. In Lucknow: the Maharaja of Samthar; the Raj Mata of Mehmoodabad; the Raja and Rani of Mehmoodabad; the Raja of Jahangirabad. In Rajasthan: Raj Mata Gayatri Devi of Jaipur; Maharaja Gaj Singh of Jodhpur; the Nawab and Begum of Loharu; Thakur and Kanwar Rani of Diggi. In New Delhi: Begum Mehtab Zamani Ali Khan of Rampur; Princess Sita of Kapurthala.

For the invaluable help, cooperation, and information that each gave, I am indebted to these people. In London: Sir Robin Mackworth-Young, Her Majesty's Librarian, Royal Library, Windsor Castle; Robert Skelton, Victoria and Albert Museum; Professor Nirad Chaudhuri; Mark Zebrowski; John Saumurez-Smith; Gita Mehta; Marianne Velmanns; Jeanne Forte. In the United States: Woodman Taylor, Fogg Art Museum, Harvard; Weston Naef, J. Paul Getty Museum; Paul F. Walter; James Ivory; Ismail Merchant; John Kenneth Galbraith and Katherine Atwater Galbraith; Edwin C. Binney III; Raghubir Singh; Terry Abbott; Stephen Jamail; Lee Nasso. At Air India: Mrs. Pallavi Shah; Betty Seidenwand. At Doubleday: Alex Gotfryd; Albert Yokum; Claire Giobbe; Shaye Areheart; Victoria Cherney; Susan Sandler; Melanie Greco. To the following, my deepest thanks. For their professional expertise in photographing the art work: Nicholas Vreeland; Rick Stafford, Photographic Services of the Fogg Art Museum, Harvard. For her erudition in compiling the Costume Glossary: Edith Gilbert Welch. For his tirelessness and sensitive graphic design: Michael Flanagan. For his enthusiastic, constant, and informed guidance throughout this entire project: Stuart Cary Welch, Curator of Islamic and Later Indian Painting at the Fogg Art Museum, Harvard, Special Consultant in charge of the Department of Islamic Art at the Metropolitan Museum of Art. For her original inspiration and always unique insight: Diana Vreeland, Special Consultant to the Costume Institute of the Metropolitan Museum of Art.

Jacqueline Kennedy Onassis
September 1985

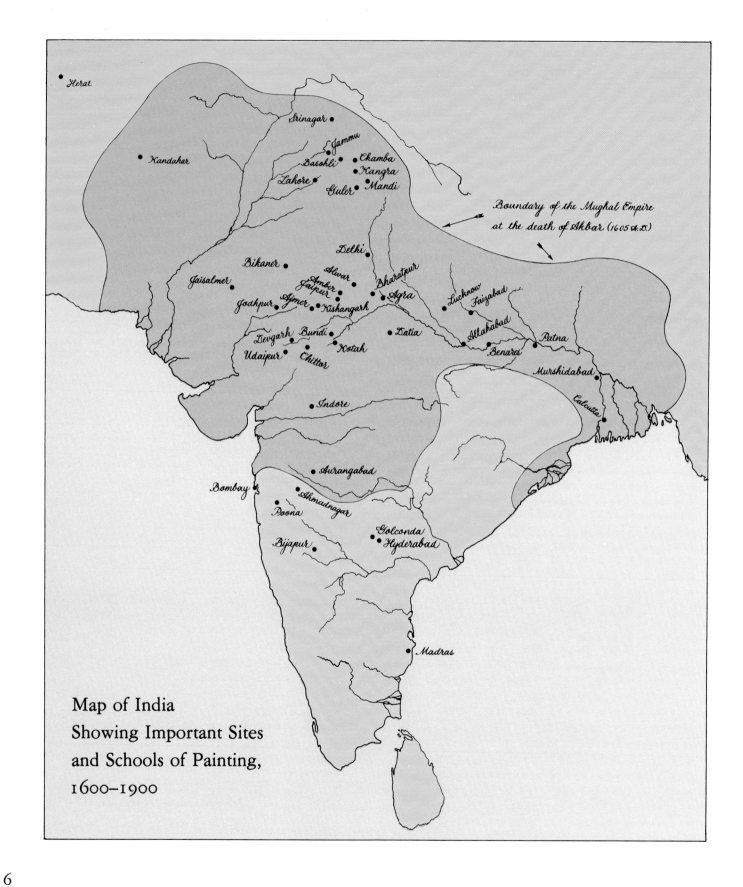

Herat

Kandahar

Srinagar

Jammu

Basohli
Chamba
Kangra
Lahore
Guler
Mandi

Boundary of the Mughal Empire
at the death of Akbar (1605 A.D.)

Delhi

Bikaner
Alwar
Bharatpur
Jaisalmer
Amber
Jaipur
Agra
Lucknow
Faizabad
Jodhpur
Ajmer
Kishangarh
Allahabad
Patna
Devgarh
Bundi
Datia
Benares
Udaipur
Kotah
Murshidabad
Chittor
Calcutta

Indore

Aurangabad

Bombay
Ahmadnagar
Poona
Golconda
Bijapur
Hyderabad

Madras

Map of India
Showing Important Sites
and Schools of Painting,
1600–1900

Contents

Introduction

Americans have for centuries felt spiritual kinship with India. The world's two largest democracies, we share a common colonial heritage. Trade with England brought Indian objects into our homes long before the Boston Tea Party—the tea for which came via India. Indian ideas contributed profoundly to our heritage. Emerson, the quintessential wise American, and Whitman, one of our greatest poets, found inspiration in Indian thought. Gandhi, influenced by Thoreau's "Civil Disobedience," combined it with his own philosophy of nonviolence drawn from Indian religious tradition. In turn, Martin Luther King, Jr., emulated Gandhi in his nonviolent crusade for civil rights. India's contributions to mathematics, science, religion, and art have been as essential to American culture as to that of the rest of the world.

On a more personal level, friendships between Indians and Americans can be traced back to the seventeenth century. Americans who visited India as merchants usually returned intrigued by the country and with warm feelings for the people. Fascination with India first affected Americans centuries ago—long before Yankees sawed ice from the river at Gardiner, Maine, ingeniously insulated it with sawdust, and stacked it as ballast in their trading vessels. Months later, having used the chilly cargo to refrigerate food and cool the area, they sold it in Calcutta, at a considerable profit, which was recycled into yard goods and spices.

As the most exotic, varied, remote, and hospitable place in the world where one can manage by speaking English, India has long been not only a wondrous resource for travelers but also for those who consider themselves more serious—people who roam the world in search of infinite varieties of music and art, folkloristic survivals, or some new hybrid of the *Gloriosa superba*. For those blessed with fanatical curiosity, however rarified the topic, India has provided—and continues to provide—sympathetic colleagues.

One such Indo-American friendship takes us to the origin of this book, which was sparked in a car while we were driving through the old quarter of Jaipur to see Ved Pal Sharma, known as Bannu—the most talented Indian artist now working in the tradition of miniature painting. We were traveling in India in connection with the 1985 Festival of India, exploring possibilities for exhibitions, particularly one for the Metropolitan Museum's Costume Institute. Court dress was on our minds, and we realized the need for an introductory book, illustrating the dazzling clothes of India's Hindu and Muslim courts and providing background material to a field little known even by "experts."

Conveniently, our car contained the requisite talent for the project. Jacqueline Kennedy Onassis, of Doubleday & Company, had long been interested in India and had edited other books associated with the Costume Institute. Sitting in the front seat was a witty Indian friend, Naveen Patnaik, who knows a great deal about Indian history and life without having taken advanced degrees or burdened the world with footnotes. Naveen had grown up among those who wore the sort of costumes for which we searched. Not himself a Rajput, he was on intimate terms with many former princely families, and he fascinated us with humorous, sometimes poignant anecdotes of the old days. His insider's knowledge enabled him to write the text that follows. Edith Welch, my wife, provided another necessary ingredient. A student of costumes, she worked for many years in the Department of Textiles of the Museum of Fine Arts, Boston, where she did almost everything but try them on. To her, we owe the glossary. As a devotee of India and Indian arts, I was able to suggest visually exciting and appropriate paintings and old photographs for the book and to introduce them to the readers.

Our enthusiasm for the project mounted as we drove into the busy little Jaipur square from which we would walk through narrow streets to Bannu's house. Halfway down an alleyway, we realized that he, too, should be invited to contribute to the publication. A book was launched.

Alerted by his sixth sense of our arrival, Bannu greeted the chattering bibliophiles in front of his door. He is a tall, thin gentleman in his late forties who lives with his family in a venerable whitewashed stone town house. Through massive wooden doors, one enters a simple square court or atrium, open to the sky, from which a narrow staircase leads to the four floors above. Neither large nor small, this elegantly simple house has belonged to Bannu's family at least since the early nineteenth century. Except for the addition of such amenities as electricity and a few newly glazed windows in Bannu's studio cum living room, it has never been altered.

Visiting Bannu is enjoyable and enlightening, for he keeps sparkingly alive an almost lost traditional Indian art. More than anyone else, he has shown me how Indian miniatures, such as those illustrated here, were created. Before we met many years ago, I was told that he was not only a remarkably gifted artist and one of the few in India who continued to work in the traditional technique of miniature painting, but that his knowledge of Rajput and Mughal pictorial styles and of costume, arms and armor, and architecture was on a par with that of the most knowledgeable connoisseurs and scholars. Since then, I have spent many hours sitting beside him, watching the intricate development of a picture from the bare, unprepared paper to the final burnishing.

In Bannu's house, painting is a performance—just as it must have been in the glorious days of the Mughal and Rajput court ateliers. While at work, he receives visitors —connoisseurs, dealers, and various cronies, who applaud his virtuosic brushstrokes as if he were some master musician playing a particularly beautiful *alap,* or prelude. The clublike atmosphere is further enriched by music, usually from a phonograph. And it is characteristically Indian that Bannu welcomes things that we in our foreign preciousness damn as impure or inappropriate. Bannu's music-to-paint-to ranges from ragas performed on the vina to the cloying elevator-treacle of Mantovani's massed violins. His costumes vary from almost immaculate white *kurtas* (shirts) and *paijamehs* to comfortable *lungis* (towel-like wraparounds) printed in patterns borrowed from the immortal canvasses of Jackson Pollock (Fig. I A).

Over the years, I have spent many hours diligently interviewing this latter-day Indian master. Somewhere, I have notes tracing his ancestors, many of whom were artists of the Jaipur court, whose supply of superb pigments (many of them ground from semi-precious stones) he has inherited. From time to time, Bannu delights me by rummaging in a closet for portfolios of drawings and paintings by his ancestors. Among them is a sensitive self-portrait by a great-great-grandfather, painted in newfangled English water-color washes during the days of Maharaja Ram Singh II (ruled 1835–80), the last great traditional patron of his dynasty. Inasmuch as Indian painters usually stemmed from artist families who passed down bundles of *materia technica* (sketches and half-finished paintings, their stock-in-trade of motifs), Bannu's artistic legacy was no surprise.

The surprises emerged as I watched him work. A happy one was Bannu's burnishing stone, a marvelously smooth coffee-colored slab that would thrill any connoisseurly Japanese. Onto it, at various stages, he places his work in progress, painted side down, to be gently but firmly stroked with a pleasingly hand-fitting rounded agate. An artist's tools are almost as appealing as his pictures.

Bannu began his demonstration of the painting of a miniature by selecting a piece from his hoard of old, handmade papers. He then primed it with an evenly brushed wash of white pigment, taken from one of the clam shells (the traditional containers of pigments in India and Iran) lined up beside his painting board—a plastic one, adorned with fake woodgrain! After the white primer had dried, a rapid process during the desiccating Jaipur winter, he gave it a first burnishing, which locked the pigment into the fibers of the paper and made the surface invitingly smooth to the brush. My artist friend then asked me to choose a subject. Aware of Bannu's style, I suggested that a pretty girl would be welcome, at which he reached for a book written by one of my former students and turned to an illustration of a dancing-girl painted at Kotah, in Rajasthan, in about 1840. After propping the book in front of him, he set to work, deftly brushing in the girl's outline with almost invisible, grayed-down black pigment. Covering over displeasing lines with white and gradually darkening the pigment, Bannu brought the nautch girl to life. While she took form, I noted Bannu's hands, characteristically an artist's—or surgeon's—with long, thin, sensitive but strong fingers. The picture grew slowly and methodically. At last satisfied with the underdrawing, Bannu put aside the book from which —in the traditional way—he had taken his theme. He began to improvise. Occasionally he turned to me for suggestions, for I played the traditional role of patron. If I ordained that the painted girl smile, flirt, scowl, or wear a certain kind of jewel she did so—with a little help from obliging Bannu.

Three quarters of an hour later, Bannu progressed from grisaille to color, concentrating first on one part of the picture, then another. Bit by bit, very slowly, the girl emerged as from a dense mist. Cheeks gained roundness and pinkness, the slightly petulant but smiling red lips took on personality, necklaces and earrings began to sparkle, and her hair became lustrously black. From time to time, burnishing interrupted the brushwork, enhancing and unifying the composition as varnish does an oil painting. Artist and patron were lost in time.

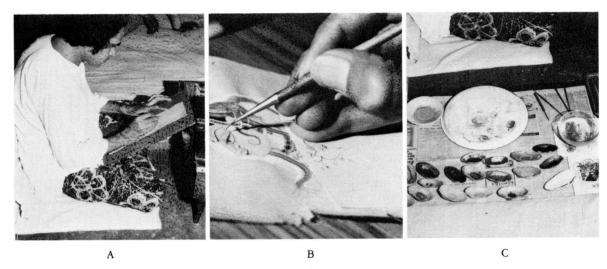

A   B   C

Fig. 1. *Bannu, the Jaipur Miniaturist, at Work.* Stuart Cary Welch, 1979.

Do miniature painters use magnifying glasses? The old, recurring question was answered. Yes, Bannu has one, for especially fine detailing. He also uses a scrap of paper on which to rest the side of his hand for steadiness while working (Fig. 1B), and he shapes the point of his brush by testing it on another scrap, where squiggles of color gather as the picture develops. The back of his hand provides a convenient palette to blend subtle shades of color. Other tools and materials are brought out as required. Gold pigment, made by grinding up gold leaf, drab in its little clam shell (Fig. 1C), is applied in even drabber looking washes, which fire up like switched-on light bulbs when touched with a finely pointed, but smooth, burnishing tool. To paint pearls, he applies whites in thick impasto, using a special binding medium of dark resin mixed with the pigment and applied in viscous little globs. These may be built up into high relief by repeated applications, and gold ornaments gain richness by additional layers of the precious metallic pigment. Just before the final burnishing, Bannu adds glitter to the gold by gently pricking and striating the surface with a steel needle set into a pencil-like wooden handle.

Another recurrent question: how long does it take to paint a miniature? The answer, perhaps, can be estimated from the fact that Bannu's Kotah girl, a single, partly finished figure, approximately three inches from head to midriff, required five hours of work. An illustration to one of the Mughal Emperor Akbar's historical manuscripts bears a note from the artist saying that he painted it in fifty days.

To understand Indian culture one must shed rigid views of time and space. On arrival in New Delhi, stepping from the plane, I breathe in a strange, not disagreeable aroma. It evokes ideas and excites the senses. Thousands of years ago Aryan invaders probably noted the same mysterious scent, and in the mid-seventeenth century, Shah Jahan, returning to his capital, may have had a whiff and halted his procession of elephants to investigate it. Like me, perhaps, he recognized the smoky element as burning cow dung, a readily available fuel in a land crowded with deeply respected, indeed revered, cows. What I inhale is wafted from cooking fires in myriad households across New Delhi's great sprawl.

An infinitesimal part of the tang could be ascribed to other cuisines, those enjoyed by the more elevated and rarified people with whom we are particularly concerned in this book. For them, a touch of smokiness adds nuances to far less spartan dishes, gastronomic triumphs requiring hours of preparation, to be consumed in a trice—followed by wistful, satisfied smiles.

Eyes, ears, nose, and perceptions of taste and touch are catalyzed in India. Sights or sounds that would bore at home fascinate there. On an Indian street, in a railway station, or surrounded by some scrubby landscape, day or night I remain keenly alert.

But let us turn to a more artful scent, available at an old-fashioned perfumery in Chandni Chawk, the market street opposite the Mughal Emperor Shah Jahan's Red Fort in Old Delhi. By far the best-smelling store in the world, it is also exceptionally friendly. On arriving from the hurly-burly of the street, one sees the gentleman in charge sitting behind a simple counter, near a splendid early eighteenth-century fitted coffer of teak, inlaid with ivory trees and flowers. Its partitions hold many small, cut-glass bottles partly filled with thick honey and amber colored liquids, traditional scents concocted according to ancient formulas. The shopkeeper, presumably a descendant of the founder, decants them with magicianly skill, trickling the precious liquids into tiny bottles, which an assistant packs into colorful cardboard boxes. While I enjoy the nostalgia, sample the stock of attars—some made from flowers, others from the glands of musk deer, woods, and earths—interruptions occur, customers to buy sandalwood soap, scented hair oil, or *dhoop* (incense). I particularly enjoyed the visit of an old boulevardier, who paid a rupee (about ten cents) for a bit of cotton touched with *gill* (made from dew collected from a special earth at just the right time of year). After tucking it into a fold of his ear, he wandered off, to meet with his beloved.

Whenever I visit Gulab Singh Johri Mal, I learn more about these oil-based perfumes, which are far longer lasting than the more volatile alcohol-based French ones. I cherish several bottles from early nineteenth-century Hyderabad or Lucknow. Their amberlike contents are rock hard, but the mysterious smell lingers, strong as ever, whisking one to ghostly soirees.

The bottled nostalgia from the Chawk exemplifies a basic Indian activity: the exploration of both the mundane and the spiritual, which they have done more thoroughly and deeply than any other people. One is awed by their contributions to religion—Buddhism, Hinduism, Indian Islam, and many others—but how marvelous it is that unlike most of us they know that the worldly and otherworldly can meet and join. Asceticism doubtless has its rewards; but one might suggest, very humbly, that such rarified experiences as wearing sackcloth and ashes or living on a single grain of rice per day are not for everyone. Spiritual heights can be approached by other routes.

A favorite one is art, by which I refer not just to painting, sculpture, and architecture, but to the intangible, living arts that cannot be framed, mounted on pedestals, or sewn between book covers: the arts of life—spontaneous dance, conversation, cookery, massage, perfumery, horsemanship (and elephantmanship!), the making and wearing of clothes and adornments, rituals, parades, festivals. . . . The list is endless. And all these ephemera contribute to other arts, especially to painting. The reader may now wish to turn from the text to the pictures, exploring not only their outer subjects—the portrait, building, or hunting scene—but also the extraordinary, almost hidden details, figures in backgrounds, jewels, bibelots and furniture, and textiles.

In India, life is lived to the fullest, as is apparent in the miniatures and photographs assembled here, whatever their period or style. As interpreted by Indian artists and photographers, people, animals, and settings often are seen with the heightened intensity we associate with grand opera. Elephants do not amble, they hurtle forward with the might and power of express trains; birds do not fly, they soar or cut the air in swooping arabesques; and a pair of pajamas such as is worn by the Nawab of Chawnepor, a cross between a soufflé and a rolling landscape, was designed with such élan that their wearer would have stolen the scene from Othello during the final act of Verdi's tragedy. But if one senses extraordinary, highly charged style in these pictures, one also finds deep sensitivity to human frailty, loving tenderness, sweet familiality, and profound piety.

Zest, verve, and enthusiasm permeate Indian life and Indian art. Indian patrons have spurred artists and craftsmen on with infectious excitement. No effort, no expense, no amount of time has been spared. Whole complexes of temples were hewn out of boulders or mountainsides. Traditionally, what might seem to us minor tasks were approached with the seriousness of crusades. Many months of the most painstaking, blinding toil went into the creation of a Dacca muslin shirt or sari so diaphanous and fragile that it could be worn only once. And no one pointed a guilt-producing finger at those who basked in overt luxury. On the contrary, crowds gathered—and still gather—to share the wearer's pleasure and to applaud his or her good fortune.

In India, festivals great and small are constant. "What a *tamasha!*" an Indian will say, bubbling over with delight at almost anything enjoyable that moves. Lack of motion, the static, usually suggests death, or at least dullness and unhealthiness. To an Indian, bathing in a tub of still water is unthinkable.

Indians are deeply conscious of roles in life. A king should look like a king, even if he is unable to behave like one; and everyone else, from the queen to the prime minister, princes and princesses, musicians, dancing-girls, and the special servant who cleans up after elephants, should also be true to their stations. The portraits assembled here all follow this rule. Important people, such as the two stately, if dour, gentlemen seated on a Victorian-Indian bench (Pl. 68) are fittingly attired, and their expressions accord with the imposing furniture of the *haveli* (mansion). In our culture, Mussolini, for example, chin jutting and corners of the mouth lowered in dictatorial disdain, grasped this simple and reasonable rule. Most of us hold our breaths, mouth the photographer's mantra ("cheeeese"), and muster counterfeit smiles.

The majestic look striven for at the courts of maharajas and nawabs was achieved by living the good life and avoiding inappropriate activities: walking, running, or indulging in exercise after twenty—except, of course, for hunting, polo, and lovemaking.

In courtlier days, working was scorned, especially when it involved physical effort.

INTRODUCTION

Writing poetry and composing music were tolerated, but traditional, artistically minded princes employed others to paint pictures for them. Being the patron of a school of painting or music was worthier than mastering the brush or playing an instrument, although it was acceptable to paint or play music unprofessionally. There were, of course, a few outstanding exceptions: rajas or sultans so burning with artistic aspiration that their talents found expression. With the arrival in India of the camera, which did not require physical exertion, an exciting artistic outlet reached princely courts. Several maharajas, including Ram Singh II of Jaipur, took to the lens as mallards to a marsh. Boldly manning the shutter, they took photographs of great distinction.

The miniature paintings and photographs illustrated here date from the sixteenth through twentieth centuries. Rooted in popular culture, from which they draw much of their energy, they were made for the rulers and their circles. Examples from three major artistic flowerings are included: the Muslim Mughal dynasty (1526–1858); the Hindu Rajput courts, represented here from the seventeenth century onward; and the British period, from the eighteenth through the twentieth centuries.

The Mughal emperors were Muslims, disciples of the Prophet Mohammed. Although Arab merchants were the first Muslims in India, and they were soon followed by Arab soldiers, who conquered Sind in A.D. 712, the Muslim arts of India were far more strongly influenced by Turks, Afghans, and Persians. In the eleventh century, Mahmud of Ghazna, a Turk (Ghazna, his capital, is between Kabul and Kandahar in Afghanistan), raided northwest India and conquered the Punjab, India's strategic gateway from the northwest. In the twelfth century, Mahmud's successors gave way to another dynasty of Turks, the Ghurids, who soon spread widely across northern India, or Hindustan. They dominated many of the local Hindu rajas and landlords, who had little choice but to cooperate with them. Although their leaders, the sultans—hence the term Sultanate Period—were foreigners, of Turkish and Persian background, India as always conquered the conquerors by Indianizing them. Their music and literature were strongly influenced by indigenous traditions, and their art and architecture were transformed by the local, often Hindu, craftsmen, even though they were usually directed by masters from the heartlands of the Islamic world.

Babur, "the Tiger," the first Mughal Emperor, was born in 1483 in Ferghana, a minor principality north of the Hindu Kush mountains. Descended from both Timur and

Chinghiz (Genghis) Khan, his lineage far exceeded his inheritance. Life held little promise when, at the age of eleven, he inherited an insecure throne, almost empty coffers, and a small cadre of followers. But the Tiger was ambitious, intelligent, and charismatic, and his people were sturdy and loyal. Babur learned strategy, tactics, swordsmanship, and all other essential arts as a boy, aspiring to retake Samarkand and his ancestral domains. His education included victories and defeats; by 1513 he had captured Kabul, but it was evident that his future lay to the southeast. In 1517, aware that the Lodi sultans were in opulent disarray, he raided India. By 1526, Babur had conquered the Punjab, and in the spring of 1526, at Panipat, near Delhi, Babur's well-disciplined small army and artillery routed Sultan Ibrahim Lodi's far greater force, after terrifying his hundred war elephants with the unfamiliar roars of cannon.

If the Mughal dynasty owes its existence to Babur, so does much of its culture, as exemplified by the first Emperor's lively and elegantly written memoirs, the *Baburnama.* This lengthy, candidly personal, fascinating book is already imbued with Mughal poetic naturalism. Babur's sensitive love for nature in all its forms, his sharply observant eyes, statesmanly talents, wit, dynamism, and earthy solidity all reemerge in the magnificent new artistic synthesis of Mughal India. Sadly, he died in 1530, too soon to have established clearly defined patterns of government or culture. Babur's only tangible artistic heritage consists of a few ruined buildings and scarcely traceable gardens. His eldest son, Humayun (ruled 1530–1556), who inherited the throne at twenty-three, was far less vigorous and outgoing than Babur. He was also less successful. His subtle intelligence and soldierly talents were too often outweighed by aristocratic languor and indulgence in the family weakness for opium and wine. As a result, this sensitive visionary, who preferred the arts of peace to those of war, was forced from India by a former Mughal officer, ambitiously effective Sher Shah Afghan, whose talents for government were later beneficial to the Mughals.

After bleak and desperate wanderings in Sind, Humayun was given sanctuary by Shah Tahmasp, the Safavid ruler of Persia, an episode of great consequence for Mughal art. He was received at the Safavi court when Shah Tahmasp had lost interest in a subject to which he had been deeply and creatively devoted: painting. Humayun was shown brilliant miniatures by the shah's artists, to whom he was also introduced. As might be expected, the Mughal Emperor especially admired artists who painted naturalistically, in styles reminiscent of Babur's prose style. Inasmuch as the shah's patronage was on the wane, Humayun's enthusiasm held promise of employment at the Mughal court, once it had been reestablished. At this juncture, ill-starred Humayun's fortunes began to improve. Shah Tahmasp offered arms and funds; in 1545, Humayun recovered Kandahar. Before long, he had also taken Kabul, where by arrangement he was joined by several of Shah Tahmasp's masterful artists, who then founded the school of Mughal painting as we know it. While there, Humayun learned of Sher Shah Afghan's death and of his successor's vulnerability. In 1555, he reoccupied Delhi and Agra.

But Humayun's luck did not hold. In 1556, he died after tripping on the massive stone stairs of his library, built by his late enemy Sher Shah Afghan. Once again, the fate of the Mughals rested on the shoulders of a boy—Prince Akbar, who was barely thirteen.

Akbar, known as "the Great" (ruled 1556–1605), refounded the Mughal Empire. Even more dynamic than his grandfather, he is usually ranked with Asoka as one of India's greatest rulers, a true philosopher-king. Whether one judges him as conqueror, statesman, hunter, raconteur, theologian, host, or patron, he was wizardly. If there is truth to the claim that he never learned to read or write, the failing did not prevent him from commissioning a vast and wonderful library. For him, life was lived on a grand scale. His conquests encompassed all of northern and central India. Seemingly at whim, with demonic speed, he built great urban complexes. Poets, holy men, philosophers, architects, and every sort of artist or craftsman flocked to his court, from all of India and the Islamic world and beyond. Fascinated by people and ideas and requiring very little sleep, he gathered wise men who met with him all night.

Akbar realized that his empire was weakened by religious diversity and tried to unify it. To link himself with the rulers of India's Hindu principalities, he took wives from the royal houses of the Rajputs. This not only further Indianized his dynasty, but also brought powerful Rajput officers and armies into the imperial fold. Orthodox Muslims were often shocked by the Emperor's seeming heresies and by his close friendships with Hindus. His tolerance extended even to his sternest critic, Badaoni, who was generously but pointedly assigned a major project: the translation into Persian of a Hindu epic, for distribution to his fellow Muslims—another of Akbar's attempts to bridge the gap between the empire's two major religious communities.

As a patron of painting, Akbar fulfilled the underlying attitudes of Babur's autobiography. Like our news photographers, artists accompanied the Emperor and his armies, sketching people and events as history unfolded. A marvelous series of illustrated historical manuscripts was prepared for him, the most vital and immediate of which was the *Akbarnama,* the history of his own reign, written by his worshipful friend Abu'l Fazl (see Pl. 1). Boldly composed, in bright colors and with surging rhythms that seem to emanate from the Emperor's own vitality, these reportorial miniatures are peopled by accurately observed portraits. A humble but attentive courtier (see Pl. 3), the perfect servant, standing before the Emperor as though awaiting an order, was scrutinized and painted for another of Akbar's projects, a portrait album formed so that "those that have passed away have received new life, and those who are still alive have immortality promised them" *(A'in-i-Akbari,* p. 115).

Akbar's eldest son and successor, who took the name Jahangir ("the World-Seizer") after inheriting the throne in 1605, was a ruler-aesthete who doted on painting and beautiful objects of art. Fortunately, the Mughal throne had been so solidly secured by his father that he could pursue his artistic, spiritual, and other inclinations in tranquility. A lover of all good things, he was also energetic, curious, and quirky. His memoirs, the *Tuzuk-i-Jahangiri,* are as personal as his great-grandfather Babur's, with almost day-to-day notes on what he did, thought, saw, commissioned, was given, gave, and bought. He described his dreams, noted the miraculous raising of a boy from the dead, and pondered the occasion when a tiger "by way of sport, and not with the idea of rage . . . threw [a naked yogi] on the ground and began to behave to him as it would to his own female." Ordinarily kind to animals, he once observed an elephant shivering at its bath and ordered that the water be warmed. Yet he could be imperiously cruel, as when he forced a disloyal son to review his partisans tidily impaled on rows of stakes. As a patron, Jahangir was far more of a connoisseur than his father. On reaching the throne, he dismissed most of his father's numerous artists, maintaining only those who met his notably refined standards. He was also an enthusiastic collector, whose albums included excellent European prints set in superb Mughal floral borders and whose palaces contained niches filled with Chinese porcelains.

The early Mughal emperors' invariable willingness to face reality was expressed by Jahangir in confessional accounts of his weaknesses, which ranged from overly zealous hunting expeditions to wine and opium. Miniatures from his official history of the reign show him jowly and bleary-eyed, honest portrayals for which one respects him all the more. On reading his memoirs, studying his paintings, and admiring the daggers, wine cups, and other objects made for him, one admires Jahangir increasingly, as a lover of art, of life, and as a deeply humane person. An illustration to the poet Sa'di's *Bustan* ("The Garden") depicts a feast given by generous Hatim T'ai, who ordained that his finest horse be slaughtered and cooked to feed unexpected guests (Pl. 4). Although this legendary episode occurred in Arabia, Jahangir's painter set it in Mughal India. Every detail, from the guests to the tents, cooks, utensils, food, and table manners, was accurately portrayed from goings-on at the imperial court.

Shah Jahan (ruled 1628–1658) was more passionate about architecture and jewelry than about painting, although magnificent pictures were painted for him. Remembered as "the Great Mughal," his reign furthered the trends toward formality and classicism. His palaces at Agra, Lahore, and Delhi achieved new heights of aristocratic elegance and grandeur. Although Mughal floral ornamentation can be traced back at least to Akbar's reign, under Shah Jahan it was so prevalent that gatherings at court resembled botanical gardens—except that the flowers were of semiprecious stones set into white marble and were woven, embroidered, or carved from rubies and emeralds.

One senses, however, that a true romantic occupied the stately Peacock Throne, which could only have been commissioned by a devoted lover of art. Behind the grandeur and formality was Shah Jahan the sensitive, creative, intense dreamer, whose beloved wife Mumtaz Mahal died while bearing her fourteenth child. It was she for whom he built one of the world's most moving—and extravagant—buildings, the Taj Mahal, the magic of which can be resisted only by determinedly "serious" architectural historians. The measure of Shah Jahan's devotion is also apparent from other touching episodes, such as the six months he spent personally nursing a daughter who had been severely burned when her clothing brushed a candle by which she was reading a manuscript.

Shah Jahan's paradise was flawed by the recurrent Mughal disorder: problems of succession. Just as Jahangir had conspired for Akbar's throne, and Shah Jahan himself for Jahangir's, so did Prince Aurangzeb plot to occupy his father's. His opportunity came when Shah Jahan developed a serious, not very royal disorder: strangury. Although Dara Shikoh had been appointed Crown Prince and had access to the imperial armies and treasure, Aurangzeb was more effectively ambitious. While Dara spent most of his time at court with his father and devoted himself to religion and the arts, Aurangzeb learned military tactics and strategy. Combining deviousness with soldierliness, Aurangzeb defeated Dara and his other brothers; by 1658 he had imprisoned his father in Agra fort and replaced him as Emperor.

Akbar's enlightened policies, which had lent the empire stability and strength, were discarded one by one. Although the Muslim imperial family had intermarried with Hindu Rajput families, and the veins of Aurangzeb himself pulsed with Rajput blood, he weakened most of the links to the princes of Hindustan. To support never-ending campaigns in the Deccan and elsewhere, he taxed non-Muslims, and his pious but unforgiving nature further strained relations with many of his ablest Rajput officers. Before dying a very old man in 1707, he was tormented by the knowledge that his fierce efforts had brought not triumphs but weakness. The empire never recovered.

Between 1707 and 1748, more Mughals occupied the throne than during all the empire's earlier history. Gradually, the empire was weakening. In 1739, the Peacock Throne itself was carried off, along with masses of other loot, by the Persian adventurer Nadir Shah. Previously loyal governors established virtually independent states, to which they attracted many of the emperors' ablest poets, dancers, and artists.

During the second half of the eighteenth century, the legend of Mughal wealth and the reality of Mughal feebleness continued to attract ambitious outsiders. Like tigers fighting over a bullock, British, French, and other eager powers struggled for India. Lord Clive and his successors won, and in due course India became the "jewel" of the British Empire.

Although weakened politically, the Mughals, centered at Delhi, somehow kept their legend alive. Rajput princes, Muslim nawabs, and foreigners still paid fealty to the throne, which was now but a gilded counterfeit.

The dynasty founded by a poet ended with one—Bahadur Shah II (ruled 1837–1858), who was exiled to Burma by the British after the India Mutiny of 1857. A patron of the great Ghalib, often considered the preeminent Mughal poet, he continued to compose verse from a tawdry cot in Rangoon, and to him are ascribed the tragic words comparing his lot to "a handful of dust." Mughal culture long outlasted the empire.

Without the Rajputs, the proud warriors and rulers of the kshatriya caste who settled in northern India's plains and hills, the Mughal Empire and Mughal culture would have been very different and of brief duration. Descended from Aryans, Huns, Scythians, and various Central Asian ancestors as well as from indigenous roots, the Rajputs were so loyal to their separate clans that they rarely joined together, even against a common enemy. United, they could have swept the Mughals from the land. Separately, they became feudatories of the Mughal emperors, serving the empire as officers and frequently providing wives to the imperial household.

Among the Rajput houses, those of Amber and Bikaner were especially close to the Mughals, both militarily and matrimonially. Raja Man Singh of Amber and Rai Singh of Bikaner were trusted friends of Akbar. Other Rajputs followed the example of the Rana of Mewar, their senior nobleman, who traced his ancestry to the sun. He stoutly held out against imperial control from his great citadel at Chittor, and it was not until a century or so later that Mewar's art—always a telling symptom—yielded to imperial influences.

Both chivalrous and romantic figures, the Rajput princes were protectors of Hinduism as well as soldiers and rulers. Traditionally, they lived in mighty fortresses, large enough not only to house their families, retainers, and elephants and other livestock, but also to protect their villagers at times of siege. Often set atop strategic citadels, they were virtually impregnable, self-sufficient complexes with temples and shrines, storage areas for grain and water, large stables, kitchens, a treasury, and workshops of all sorts, each staffed with custodians as well as craftsmen and artists.

Living quarters were divided into two separate sections; the *mardana* for the men and the *zenana* for the women and children. The former included a capacious durbar hall, for formal gatherings of the full court and guests, chambers for private audience, and open courtyards, often with gardens. The *zenana* was an enclosed maze of a world, often guarded by eunuchs, with its own gardens and public rooms as well as private apartments. The larger Rajput establishments maintained staffs of entertainers: musicians, puppeteers, nautch (dancing) girls, and—after 1885—a theatrical troop, all under the direction of a special functionary of the court.

By the seventeenth century, Rajputs cultivated war as a fine art. Boys, and sometimes girls, learned swordsmanship, tactics, and marksmanship with weapons ranging from bows and arrows to matchlocks and cannon and developed talents of leadership. Military campaigns were almost annual events, usually directed against rival clansmen, who could be depended upon to adhere to the Rajput code of honor. Battle verged on ritual, at times, and it was waged with festive panache. Superbly armored, bejeweled, and crested war elephants and horses, brilliantly outfitted chiefs—sporting magnificent swords, daggers, and shields—and a virtual battalion of foot soldiers entered the field to the sound of drums and trumpets.

Most Rajput courtly activities were deeply rooted in the past. Hunting, for instance, was once a necessity: as a training ground for war, to protect the villagers from the occasional man-eating lion or tiger, and to provide food. Later, it became a sport, often with ritual overtones, although the quail, duck, and wild boar were welcome fare at Rajput feasts, noted for the excellence of the cookery.

Over the centuries, Rajput ways of life and art reflected their relationship to the central power. When the Mughals were dominant, from the mid-sixteenth through the mid-eighteenth centuries, the Rajputs were influenced by the imperial court, which in turn responded to their customs. Courtiers from Amber, Jodhpur, or Bundi, upon seeing the richly ornamented, spaciously comfortable palaces of Agra, Lahore, or Delhi, were likely to add wings or rebuild parts of their capitals, employing Mughal-trained artists and craftsmen. Rajput costume, arms and armor, textiles, and paintings also changed to imitate the prestigious, often luxurious imperial modes. Just as the Mughal Emperor's arts took motifs and ideas from other cultures—Europe, Persia, China, or Tibet—which they altered to suit their tastes, so too did the Rajputs borrow from the Mughal court. So individual were the separate Rajput styles that a Mughal motif interpreted at Amber differed greatly from the variant at Kotah, Bikaner, or Jodhpur.

With the failure of the Mughal Empire, Mughal artistic influence lessened in Rajasthan and in the Rajput states of the hills and central India. Painting, for example, became less naturalistic, regaining the powerful, simpler forms and brighter colors of pre-Mughal Rajput styles. But this renaissance of Rajput idioms was not to last; the Mughals were soon replaced by the British, whose imported architecture, paintings, and bric-a-brac came into vogue at Rajput courts.

Ralph Fitch, the first Englishman known to have reached India, arrived on foot. A late sixteenth-century embodiment of the passionately spartan English traveler, he took the overland route, and unlike most later visitors he stayed long enough to learn about the country and its ways. In 1599, preparations began for a different sort of British visitor. Determination to surpass Portuguese successes in the spice trade led to the founding of the East India Company in London. Its first venture into India brought a glut of pepper to London markets; but in 1611, the company established a profitable factory for cottons and other fabrics at Masulipatnam. From these small beginnings, the English presence in India expanded. By the late seventeenth century, Englishmen were busily trading in Madras, Calcutta, and Bombay.

Slowly, the company veered from mercantile to political power, commanding its own troops, which, led by Robert Clive, defeated the Mughal governor of Bengal at the battle of Plassey in 1757. By 1765, the East India Company was collecting taxes, and eight years later, under an act of Parliament, attained the right to administer the territories of India, under the guidance of Governor-General Warren Hastings. With astonishing speed and thoroughness, company officials were replacing the Mughals as the central figures of authority, as well as defeating such rivals as the Marathas.

If one were to list in chronological order the archetypical Britishers in India, Fitch, the mighty walker, would be followed by moderately distinguished merchants and an occasional gentlemanly emissary, such as Sir Thomas Roe, who represented King James I at the court of Jahangir. Toward the end of the seventeenth century, the British population in India expanded—and became rowdier. Clutches of Englishmen, settled near their factories, mingled cheerfully with the local people, drank toddy (a heady liqueur made from coconuts), carried on with village women and ate copious amounts of Indian food.

These hardy, informal tradesmen were replaced by more "responsible" and restrained folk in ever-increasing numbers. Not yet aware of the unhealthiness of overindulgence in hot places, few of them survived very many monsoons. But their short lives were amply rewarded, and more and more men of business went to India to make their fortunes. Soon they brought wives and families and settled in communities, mingling far less freely with Indians. English-style houses were constructed, and the British lived as though they had never left home. On the warmest days, they dressed for London, valuing dignity above comfort.

The early eighteenth century brought men eager for a share of the considerable profits. Younger sons of important merchants, even of lesser aristocrats, ventured to Madras and Calcutta, where the amenities almost compensated for the malaria. French wines, champagne, and elegant food, sometimes prepared by European chefs, were served at balls and dinner parties. Squirearchical estates were acquired by the prosperous, with staffs of servants, vast walled gardens, stables, carriages, and private barges.

As Calcutta, Madras, and later Bombay grew in importance, their British populations gained in variety and distinction. By 1770, eminent statesmen, judges, scholars, and artists as well as merchants could be found in Calcutta, Madras, and occasionally in the hinterlands. The lavishly generous Nawab of Lucknow attracted Europeans to his court, where they encouraged the ruler's revels and profited mightily from his extravagances. A stray Frenchman, General Claude Martin, settled at Lucknow and built a colossal, curiously hybrid palace, "La Martinière," which he bequeathed, along with his Calcutta house and an ample endowment, as a school for Anglo-Indian children. Like his British friends, he was impressively rich, and he collected works of art on a lavish scale. This was the time of nabobs—those who returned to England possessed of dizzying fortunes, with which they built great houses in which to entertain fashionable new friends.

Indian culture was now admired. Sir William Jones forwarded Sanskrit studies, and men such as Warren Hastings, Sir Elijah Impey, and Richard Johnson formed important collections of Indian pictures, especially of Mughal ones, which were easily understood by connoisseurs attuned to European naturalism. Patronage of the arts also thrived. Mary, Lady Impey, Sir Elijah's wife, hired three artists from Patna who had been trained in the Mughal tradition. Under her appreciative guidance, they painted a large series of natural history watercolors on English paper as well as a few portraits of her family.

This procession achieved peaks of variety and color during the late eighteenth and early nineteenth centuries. British institutions burgeoned, and church fairs, regimental teas, meetings of learned societies, hunt breakfasts, and the like transformed British India into a warmer simulacrum of the British Isles.

The early nineteenth century contains vital, pioneering figures, such as Bishop Reginald Heber, who wrote a delightfully informative *Narrative* of his journey from Calcutta to Bombay in 1824–25, and Lieutenant-Colonel James Tod, who devoted his life to Rajasthan and Gujarat. He became intimately friendly with Rajputs, whose chronicles he recorded with the help of native pundits, later to be published in volumes that remain standard works.

But prudish, smug Victorians appeared, and vital, sympathetic lovers of India were outnumbered by men of commerce and Bible-bearing dignitaries, occasionally interspersed with pleasing, comically poignant eccentrics, of the sort that enliven Britain during her dreary phases. The British presence in India, by 1850, seemed permanent—and ever-expanding.

In 1857, the India Mutiny exploded in a nightmare of blood and smashed convictions. The Indians had revolted, apparently unappreciative of the marvels of westernization, wisdom, and kindness bestowed upon them in exchange for mere worldly wealth.

In 1858, the British Crown replaced the Honorable East India Company as the government of the territories in India. The Mughal Emperor was tried and exiled to Burma. Other Indians who had mutinied were hanged, and doubtful cases shot; those who had remained loyal were rewarded. The Crown sent clusters of soldiers, judges, educators, clergymen, bankers, and tradesmen who were better disciplined—and more controlling—than ever.

In 1877, Queen Victoria was proclaimed Empress of India. Formerly independent Indian states, their princes, and citizens were now vassals of the British Empire, as were villagers, distinguished Indian academics, sadhus, fakirs, Anglicized Indian merchants, assorted "native" civil servants, and whole regiments of regional troops, bright as peacocks in their dazzling uniforms.

The Viceroy, Lord Lytton, now concluded that inasmuch as the government needed support from at least one level of society, it should be the aristocracy. Festooned with gold brocades, splattered with jewels, weighed down with gold daggers and gaudy presentation swords, and ticklish with plumes, Indian rulers mounted elephants and lent their august presences to what had been, on the whole, a comparatively earnest, dreary foreign assemblage. At last, aided by Indians, the British Empire outdazzled the Mughals.

The Indian King

Detail of Plate 45.

Several thousand years ago a group of men desiring to be kings went into the forest seeking Manu the Lawgiver, the great sage who laid the foundation of India's civilization, to ask what was required of a king. Manu replied by listing the onerous tasks of a monarch. He spoke of the harsh austerities to be practiced by a ruler. The alarmed audience watched the sky grow dark as the Lawgiver spoke of duties and made no mention of the rewards of being the highest person in the land. Finally one aspirant could control his impatience no longer and demanded to know the privileges of kingship. The Lawgiver answered, "There is but one reward for a king. Men will bow their heads to him in recognition of his merit."

This was the first lesson in monarchy taught to a royal prince. Later, the prince graduated to the study of the *Arthashastra,* the classical Indian text on government, which covered every element of administration from diplomacy to irrigation. Central to this text was the figure of the king, presiding as a four-armed father over his kingdom. With one arm he governed, with the second he provided, with the third he punished, and with the fourth he intrigued. Alas, by the eighteenth century those four arms had dwindled into one—intrigue—and Indian kings could no longer leave the bowing of men's heads to a chance recognition of merit.

(Detail) *Young King Dispensing Justice.*
From the *Gulistan* of Sa'di, ca. 1610.

29

(Detail) *Royal Procession; South Indian Raja in Palanquin.* Mid-nineteenth century.

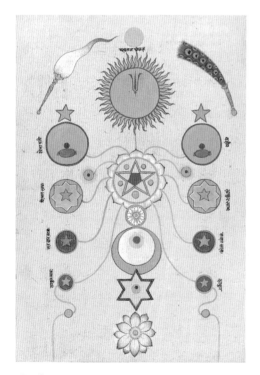

Royal Insignia.

Before an Indian maharaja entered his durbar, or hall of audience, he was preceded by rows of bare-torsoed priests chanting his lineage and tracing its origins to the pantheon of the gods themselves. Then came scholars reciting the names of the king's mortal ancestors to show his claim to the throne. They were followed by royal heralds, who shouted to the inattentive:

> Be Aware! Be Aware! There approaches the Protector of the People! The Provider of Grain! The Dispenser of Justice: The Pearl of Purity! The Diamond of Restraint! The Shadow of God on Earth!

As these monumental titles echoed through the corridors of the palace, a crash of lances striking marble floors announced the standard-bearers of the ruler's forces. Directly behind them, staff-bearers held high the symbols of monarchy. An open hand signified the seal of administration. The symbols of the Provider were the silver heads of the tiger, the elephant, the crocodile. Two staff-bearers carried a great sheaf of peacock feathers and a white horse's tail falling from a golden cone, signs of war and conquest. Last came the sword of the kingdom, symbol of implacable justice. Above the king himself was held the royal umbrella, representing the vault of the sky and his direct access to the gods. Only then, when heralds and soldiers, priests and symbols of office had raised every man to his feet and bowed every head did the eighteenth-century Indian king deign to enter his durbar hall and seat himself upon the *gaddi,* a simple cushion that was the traditional throne of the Indian monarch.

In the last flowering of Indian monarchy the whole baroque panoply of power was never more magnificently displayed—and yet the substance of power was absent. The mighty Mughal Empire had become senile. It was ruled brilliantly in the seventeenth and eighteenth centuries by a succession of outstanding emperors, but the power of the empire began leaking away after the death of the last Great Mughal, the Emperor Aurangzeb. The empire was fragmenting under the ambitions of rebellious governors who carved kingdoms for themselves in Oudh and Hyderabad. New powers, such as the Sikhs and Marathas, wrested their own empires from the chaos of crumbling imperialism. No longer restrained by an emperor's hand, older Indian kingdoms fought one another for suzerainty and survival, while mercantile Europeans raced to fill the vacuum created by Mughal decadence and enrich themselves with the fabulous wealth of India. Another hundred years would pass before frock-coated Victorians succeeded in imposing their Pax Britannica on an exhausted India and calling themselves the British Raj, but throughout those centuries of savage transition the ancient traditions of the *Arthashastra* prevailed, and an Indian ruler was still raised with the teachings of Manu .

From the moment it was known that a maharani was with child the ancient disciplines commenced. The education of the king began even before his birth, when bards gathered before the walls of the harem to sing ballads of the heroic deeds of the child's ancestors so that the unborn child would emulate such actions in his own lifetime. In the palace temple, under the guidance of the Raj Guru, or high priest, of the kingdom, prayers and sacrifices were performed to ensure the birth of a male heir. As the time of the birth approached, the women of the harem and the ruler's courtiers crowded the palace corridors. Whoever brought the news of an heir to the maharaja could ask any boon and was showered with wealth and position. Thus, the intrigue that enmeshed an Indian ruler throughout his lifetime began at his birth.

Religious Articles.

Detail of Plate 15.

As soon as the cannons were fired from the forts of the kingdom, the great celebrations that followed the birth of an heir began: nights of dancing and music, ceremonial processions in which the maharaja went on elephant-back through the capital, the feeding and clothing of the poor. Throughout these functions the Raj Guru forecast the next ruler's horoscope, calculating its periods of good fortune and ill omen.

In his early years the infant was cosseted by the ladies of the harem. His feet hardly touched the ground as he was moved from lap to lap. The only blemish on his person was the daily application of a black spot to mar his perfection and deflect the evil eye. Yet even while he was treated as a little god by the adoring harem, the infant was being educated. Toys in the shape of enameled and ivory orbs containing water, light, sand, or only air taught him about the four elements. He was given strings of the nine jewels that represented the nine planets; when he tossed them about it was as if he played with the universe itself.

When the heir was five years old he was removed from the harem and the austere regimen of the student began. Now he had to learn the epics and mythology to understand the rituals of the temple. He studied the classics, the laws of Manu, and the *Arthashastra* to understand administration and justice. He was educated in the sciences, astronomy, and mathematics, never more urgently than in the eighteenth century, when tactics and science were a necessity in war.

In a century of continuous warfare the young prince had to know how to fight on foot, on horseback, or from the howdah of an armored elephant in order to direct his forces in the field. He was taught to handle the spear, the double-bladed dagger, and the flexible sword. He was taught to wield shields made of crocodile skin and to move swiftly when encased in armor. Every weapon in use, from the bow and arrow to the cannon, had to be familiar.

Great hunts were a part of the court calendar, occasions when work and pleasure were united. The maharaja and his heir went hawking or hunted antelope with trained cheetahs, releasing them from their cages when herds of deer were sighted. There were tiger and panther hunts, and the heir showed his martial education in a peacetime approximation of the battlefield. At night he returned to a court of tents, laid out exactly like the palace itself, where the maharaja conducted administrative and political business with his rural subjects and kept himself informed of affairs in distant parts of his kingdom.

As the heir grew into manhood, two issues dominated the court: a dynastic marriage to cement the kingdom's alliance with another power and the fact that when the heir became king he would be the master and sole lover of a harem filled with maharanis and concubines. Great courtesans were the appendages of great courts. The prince was sent to these courtesans to learn manners. To the accompaniments of dance and music, they taught him to appreciate the nuances of seduction. Finally, they initiated the young man into sophisticated forms of lovemaking.

When a royal princess was found whose horoscope matched the heir's and whose lineage and dowry were impressive enough, the prince was sent on an elephant at the head of a large entourage, as if leading a conquering army to his bride's kingdom. When he returned his face was covered with a veil of flowers and mirrors winked off his bride's curtained palanquin, to deflect the evil eye. Then the palanquin disappeared into the harem, and the new bride became a part of the sequestered world of the royal women.

Less preoccupied with affairs of state than his father,

Fig. 2. (Detail) *Nautch Girls and Musicians Perform for Court Entertainment.* Late nineteenth century.

the heir was expected to take a particular interest in the arts and architecture. He built temples in accordance with ancient architectural designs. He commissioned buildings to display the genius of the kingdom's master craftsmen. This constant construction also provided employment for peasants in times of flood or drought. In the palace gardens, laid out in the Indian style, were fountains that sprinkled water during the day and scented flowers to be enjoyed in the cool after sunset. Here the heir built marble pavilions where great musicians performed through the night. These musicians had been trained in great ateliers of song and dance renowned through the whole of India.

The heir did not confine himself to life at court. In his kingdom, which was primarily agricultural, the change of seasons was celebrated with much festivity. Villagers organized cattle and horse fairs. Many sporting events took place, at which the heir played a significant role. The townspeople became familiar with him during the processions and celebrations that accompanied the frequent religious festivals.

The fulcrum of the kingdom's administration was the durbars given by the maharaja. Weekly durbars were held for the purpose of governing and dispensing justice. Ceremonial durbars celebrated royal events such as the ruler's birthday, when he was given his weight in coins by his subjects. In those turbulent times, political durbars were necessary to cement diplomatic ties with other states and, more important, to gauge the fealty of the great nobles of the land. Each *thakur,* or baron, offered a gold coin to the monarch as a token of homage, with the heir leading this ritual of loyalty.

When the maharaja died, the new king could not attend the cremation of his father. According to tradition he knelt before his father's corpse and said, "As I offer you my knee, the knees of my noblemen are pressed against the throne. I must therefore beg your leave and attend to my throne and kingdom.''

After eleven days of mourning, the new maharaja exchanged the white turban of sorrow for the red turban, which represented energy and potency. To it was pinned an aigrette in the shape of the bountiful mango. His beard was brushed in the style of his clan. He wore the close-fitting tunic and breeches of the warrior. Around his neck was a magnificent necklace studded with the nine gems that represented the nine planets. Jeweled armbands accentuated the muscular strength of his upper arms. An elaborate sash was tied around his waist as a mark of dignity. On his right foot the maharaja wore the single enameled anklet worn only by kings.

Thus appareled, he stood before the Raj Guru, who had cast his horoscope when he was born, taught him the ancient classics when he was a student, and blessed him as a bridegroom and as a warrior. Now the high priest cut his own thumb and put the *tilak,* or mark of blood, on the king's forehead to sanctify the new maharaja.

Then the Raj Guru bound the maharaja to the concept of kingship as old as India itself. Reminding the king of the words spoken by Manu the Lawgiver thousands of years ago, he recited the ancient Puranic prayer:

> May you always be zealous in performing your duties. May you always give in just measure. May you always be humble in the presence of the wise. May you always be in control of your emotions. May your zeal always be tempered by humanity. May you always be learned. May your presence always be regal. May you always possess the virtues of the divine King Rama.

Fig. 3. *Maharao Raja Roghubir Singh Bahadur of Bundi.* 1880s.

(Detail) *Maharana Jagat Singh.* Mewar, 1820.

Paintings and Photographs

Here the defeated Rajput ruler, Rao Surjan Hada, concedes defeat to the Mughal Emperor. Rajputana, the empire of the Rajput kings, is a land synonymous with valor and great sacrifice. The history of the thousand-year-old Rajput clans—descendants of the sun, the moon, and the sacred fire—is filled with tales of brave warriors on fearless steeds galloping into battle against impossible odds and legends of courageous women throwing themselves into funeral pyres rather than be dishonored by the enemy.

Rallying behind the cry "For the honor of our race and the temples of our gods!" and preceded by the pounding of their great war drums, the *nagaras,* the Rajputs rode again and again from their monumental stone forts against the foreign invader.

To the Indian, the name of Chittor Fort evokes the clash of swords and shields, the thud of the *nagaras,* and the smoke of funeral pyres where two thousand women at a time burned themselves in the act of *Jauhar,* or mass immolation, freeing their men to fall on the spears of the imperial armies battering at their walls. Crouched on the Aravalli Hills and overlooking the Thar Desert, known as the Abode of Death, the story of Chittor is one long chronicle of unbelievable sacrifice, raising its Rajputs to mythological status.

Among the many battles fought by the warriors of Chittor Fort, the early capitol of the Royal House of Mewar, perhaps this battle encapsulates the essence of Rajput chivalry. In 1303 the legendary beauty of the virtuous Queen Padmini of Chittor aroused the desire of the Afghan king, Allaudin Khilji. Determined to gain the queen, Khilji massed his armies against Chittor, placing the fortress under siege for two long years. According to lore, the Rajputs held out valiantly against the vastly superior forces of the Afghan's armies until Khilji slaughtered cows in the river that fed water to the fortress. Determined that their queen should not fall captive to the Afghan, but unable to drink water that had been polluted by the blood of sacred animals, the Rajputs of Chittor held a last council. Every person in Chittor Fort chose death over dishonor. The warriors elected to die defending their fort from armies of another faith. The women chose to burn themselves rather than be captured as prizes of war.

The British historian Colonel James Tod describes the *Jauhar* of Queen Padmini and her Rajput women in these words: "The defendants of Chittor beheld the procession of their wives and daughters, the fair Padmini closing their throng. . . . The funeral pyre was lighted . . . it closed upon them, leaving them to find security from dishonor in the devouring element."

[1.] A RAJPUT RULER SUBMITS TO EMPEROR AKBAR. MUGHAL, CA. 1590.

[2.] A MUGHAL AND A RAJPUT CONVERSE IN A GARDEN. MUGHAL, CA. 1590.

[3.] AKBAR'S COURTIER AWAITS A COMMAND. MUGHAL, CA. 1590.

[4.] THE FEAST OF HATIM T'AI. MUGHAL, 1609.

M U G H A L   P A I N T I N G

It is an Eastern custom for the host to apologize to his guests for the simplicity of his fare, even if he is offering a lavish feast attended by hundreds of people. According to the *Akbarnama,* which chronicles the reign of the Great Mughal Akbar, no less than five hundred different dishes were considered essential to the daily meals at the royal table.

A Mughal meal commenced with cool sherbets to cleanse the palate. The tastes ranged from the tangiest lemons to the sweetest watermelons, passion fruits, and pomegranates. While the nobles languidly sipped their sherbets, harassed cooks and pastry chefs and pantry boys hurriedly gave the finishing touches to a meal that had been all day in the preparation. The large variety of fish, fowls, and meats had been cooked in brass, copper, and clay pots. Now, delicacies pierced with long iron rods were lowered into the deep wells of clay ovens, watched by cooks wearing gauze masks over their faces lest a hair fall into their precious preparations. Numerous breads, from honey loaves sprinkled with poppy seeds to the *rumali roti,* the silk handkerchief bread made from wafer-thin sheets of wheat flour, were arranged on serving dishes. Vegetables were tossed in elusive spices, and cups were filled with herbal pickles to sharpen the taste buds.

A long line of servants carried the meal to the guests. Each guest was served with his own *thali,* or platter, made of gold or silver. On the platter rested a number of small containers holding the different dishes, from roasted game cooked in covered mud pits and lambs' brains and testicles swimming in mustard-leaf curry to rare and delicate vegetables such as the heart of the lotus plant. Freshwater fish, brought from the different rivers of India, or sea tortoises cooked in red chili were served next to dishes of yoghurt to cool the tongue. In the center of the platter was a mound of fragrant rice, cooked in saffron or vegetable dyes of green, purple, and red and covered with thinly beaten sheets of gold and silver.

After the guests had finished their *thalis,* attendants brought silver basins filled with leaves and poured warm water from elegant ewers as the guests washed their right hands, the hand used for eating. Fresh cloths were laid on the tables and the guests were offered sweetmeats made from carrots, marrows, pistachios, pine nuts, and rose petals, once again covered with edible gold and silver. Now came the rich variety of India's seasonal fruits—mangoes, custard apples, chikoos, mangosteens, lychees, creamy young coconuts, jackfruits, pomelos. The fruit was accompanied by tea in exquisite china cups, its fragrance enhanced with cardamoms and cloves.

[5.] WEDDING CELEBRATIONS OF PRINCE DARA SHIKOH, A.D. 1633. MUGHAL, CA. 1645.

In spite of their crowded harems, many Indian rulers were deeply devoted to their wives. Nowhere is this fact more movingly illustrated than in the lives of three successive heirs to the Mughal Empire. The Emperor Jahangir's adoration of his beautiful and talented wife led the Empress Nur Jahan to be known as the power behind the Gurganid throne. An accomplished poet, the Empress also blended perfume, traded in indigo, designed textiles, and dressed in a style of her own that set the fashion for many years. She also rode into battle, in an enclosed conveyance mounted on an elephant. She was a crack shot, shooting tigers from a veiled howdah with only the barrel of her gun exposed to the public. In the latter years of the ailing Jahangir's reign, she wielded enormous power in her husband's name. Sir Thomas Roe, England's ambassador to Jahangir's court, wrote to Prince Charles, the future King Charles I, that the Emperor's wife "governs him and wynds him up at her pleasure." On Jahangir's death, the Empress retired to Lahore, where she built a splendid mausoleum to the Emperor's memory.

Jahangir's son was the Emperor Shah Jahan. Rendered inconsolable when his cherished wife, Mumtaz Mahal, died bearing their fourteenth child, the Emperor sublimated his sorrow by building a spectacular white marble tomb to incarcerate his wife's corpse. He wished his own body to lie in a black marble tomb facing his wife's tomb so that he could mourn her loss in perpetuity. The Emperor Shah Jahan died before he could build his own mausoleum, but his wife's tomb, the Taj Mahal, remains the world's greatest monument to love.

Shah Jahan's heir, Prince Dara Shikoh, had neither power nor a magnificent monument to bestow upon his beloved wife, Nadira Banu. This ill-fated prince, defeated in a savage war of succession, was forced to flee into the desert with his wife and a handful of followers, pursued by the troops of his vengeful brother Aurangzeb. The rigors of a fugitive's life proved too harsh for his delicate wife: she died of exhaustion in his arms, asking only that she be buried in Lahore. Ignoring the danger to himself, Prince Dara Shikoh complied with his wife's dying wish and sent her body under escort to Lahore. By this act the prince further depleted his dwindling forces. He was soon captured and taken to Delhi to meet his own death. The only memorial to this doomed couple's devotion to each other is an illuminated manuscript, its pages bordered with butterflies and blossoms, bearing a simple inscription in Prince Dara Shikoh's hand to his dear wife, Nadira Banu.

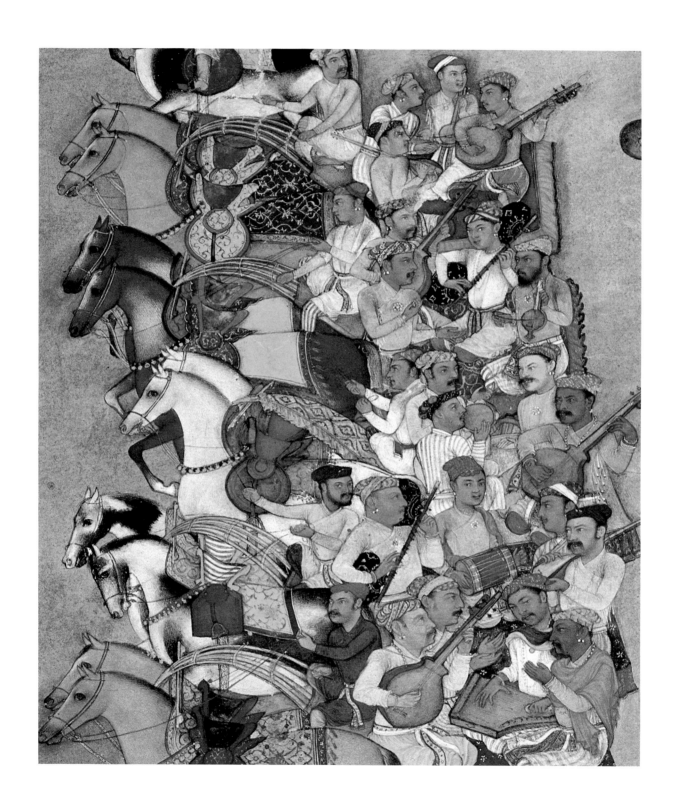

DETAIL OF PL. [5]

DETAIL OF PL. [5]

The infant Indian prince had an elaborate personal retinue—his wet nurse, who later became his foster mother, his physician, the keeper of his pets, and a host of miscellaneous attendants, such as maids and pages whose sole duty was to amuse, protect, and serve him. In the medieval courts of India there was a persistent fear of sorcery and poison surrounding the person of the heir. Food was put on pale jade plates from China ("poison plates") that turned dark if touched by any of the common poisons. The royal baby also had a personal poison-detector, sometimes an unfortunate human, more often an animal, to first taste anything he might be inclined to bite.

His toys were enameled orbs with which he could not harm himself; they contained water or light or sand or air to teach him about the four elements. He played with strings of jewels representing the nine planets, or with the soft fruits and other malleable produce of his country, every plaything designed to educate as well as divert. Even at night, when the heir retired to his cedar and sandalwood cradle strung with pearl and ruby beads, his attendants recited tales from Hindu mythology to lull him to sleep.

The production of an heir was the culmination of a mother's greatest ambitions, and royal wives went to any lengths to achieve this aim. Queens were known to induce births when there were several pregnant women in the harem to ensure their child was born first. Girl babies were smuggled out of the harem and replaced with boys so the maharani could present her husband with an heir to the throne and consolidate her own power. When the maharaja tired of her charms, the royal wife who had produced an heir retained her hold on the maharaja through his pride and fondness for her son. And when the boy himself became a ruler and ascended the kingdom's throne, a mother's power both inside and outside the harem was beyond challenge.

Oblivious to many lives affected by his welfare, the royal infant sat guarded by his mother and her coterie of women, clapping his hands with delight as he watched the court puppeteers enact the public story of his birth.

[6.] AN INFANT PRINCE. MUGHAL, CA. 1617.

[7.] IN THE BAZAARS OF SHAHJAHANABAD. MUGHAL, CA. 1645.

Delhi, capital city of numerous empires, was rebuilt a seventh time by the Mughal Emperor Shah Jahan. Known as Shahjahanabad, after its builder, the principal avenue of the new city was called Chandni Chawk, the avenue of moonlight. From the seventeenth century to the time of the British Empire, this avenue was shaded by great trees and cooled by a channel of water flowing down its center.

Lining the avenue on both sides were shops and bazaars filled with every conceivable object of luxury to appeal to the refined tastes of the Orient's richest court. Gem galleries were crowded with goldsmiths and jewelers fashioning ornaments out of fabulous stones. Bolts of Tibetan brocades, Chinese silks, muslins, and other fine fabrics from all over the world were piled to the ceilings of cloth shops. Some shops contained beautiful objects carved from jade and ivory and sandalwood while others were famous for their porcelain, china, and glass. Great chambers were piled high with carpets from Samarkand and Bukhara, and in the halls where furniture was sold, intricately carved chairs from China stood behind lines of Indian *paiyas,* or furniture legs, inlaid with gold, silver, and precious stones.

Crowds of people of every caste, race, and religion jostled one another on the wide pavements, promenading down the Chandni Chawk like a moving mosaic of the Mughal Empire. Astrologers begged to read their fortunes. Fakirs performed painful feats of asceticism as they passed. Men on the sidewalks watched the world go by as barbers shaved their faces and massaged their scalps. Turbaned guards sometimes cleared the pavements for the palanquin of a senior noble, or the members of a wedding procession brought the promenading to a momentary halt with their dancing. And the shadowy shapes of women could be seen behind the latticed balconies above the shops, watching the lively scene below.

The shopkeepers themselves, in their neat turbans and tunics, were men of prodigious wealth. The moment a courtier took off his slippers and stepped on the white sheets that covered the floor of a shop he was in the hands of men who were masters of persuasion. Wares were described in Persian couplets. Sherbets were offered. The cool, spacious interior was a relief from the noisy crowds thronging the avenue outside, and the courtier seldom left the premises without parting with a handful of gold coins in exchange for an exquisite acquisition.

[8.] AN ABYSSINIAN FROM AHMADNAGAR. MUGHAL, CA. 1633.

DETAIL OF PL. 9

[9.] SHAH JAHAN RETURNS IN TRIUMPH TO HIS FATHER, EMPEROR JAHANGIR. MUGHAL, CA. 1645.

Shah Jahan the Magnificent, born of a Hindu mother and a Hindu grandmother, was perhaps the first Mughal to think of himself as firmly rooted in Indian soil. Shah Jahan's poet laureate, Abu Talib Kalim, reflected the new Mughal attitude in his poems of India:

> One can say it is a second paradise in this respect
> Whoever leaves this garden is filled with regret.

Shah Jahan led a more settled existence than his ancestors, forgoing the informalities of the tent for a stately progress between his marble palaces at Delhi, Agra, and Lahore down a four-hundred-mile avenue shaded by enormous trees. With the increased grandeur of the Mughal Empire, Shah Jahan's days were more fixed with ceremonies than those of his father, the Emperor Jahangir. Seated on the jewel-encrusted Peacock Throne, Shah Jahan received hosts of rajas, emirs, and ambassadors. At these durbars he frequently gave gifts to the deserving, ranging from such impressive surprises as elephants in gold fetters to such delightful trifles as almonds and pistachios fashioned from gold. Turbans and robes of honor in cloth of gold, elegant daggers with precious handles in jade and gems, and the finest Kashmir shawls were other gifts from the Emperor.

A traditional ceremonial gift in recognition of valuable service to the empire was the *patka.* An elaborate sash, the *patka* was tied around the waist and a dagger was thrust into its folds. Woven from beautiful materials and perfectly finished, these sashes were carefully preserved as gifts of honor from the Mughal Emperor. Many of them still bear the seal of the imperial *toshakhana,* or treasury.

In the late seventeenth century, the last of the Great Mughals, the stern and orthodox Emperor Aurangzeb, reverted to the practice of living in tents. Like his restless forebears he spent much of his life on the battlefield, but unlike Babur this austere Emperor had to maintain a facade of imperial splendor. His camps were a city of tents embroidered in gold and silver thread and supported by painted and gilded pillars. The largest tents, with royal standards fluttering high above them, in which Aurangzeb held his imperial durbars, could be seen for miles. Smaller tents were used for council meetings. The most luxurious tents housed the ladies of the harem, their walls made of floral satin fringed with long tassels of silk. An astonished observer wrote that more than sixty elephants, two hundred camels, a hundred mules, and a hundred porters were required to carry the paraphernalia of Aurangzeb's entourage.

MUGHAL PAINTING

In strife-torn Rajputana a victorious ruler accepted the tribute of his vanquished rival. Chief among these spoils of war was his enemy's favorite dancing-girl, a courtesan renowned throughout India for her beauty. The maharaja instructed the palace eunuchs to make adequate arrangements for the courtesan to perform the *Solah Shringar,* the Sixteen Rituals of Adornment, before she was brought to him.

In the first of these rituals, maids painted intricate patterns with henna on the girl's palms and on the soles of her feet. Then herbal essences were rubbed on her body until her skin was smoother than silk. A lotus-shaped bath gushed scented water. Sandalwood was burned so that her drying tresses would absorb its fragrant incense. Cosmetics lay before a mirror: powdered *sindoor* to mark her forehead, beeswax to redden her lips, and collyrium to accentuate her long eyes. Flowing garments made of the finest cottons and silks and embroidered with delicate motifs were put on her. From a casket of jewels she chose rings for her fingers and toes, pendants for her ears, and a delicate diamond for her nose. There were bracelets and anklets and armbands, girdles for her waist and hips, collars for her neck, and gems for her hair. She completed her toilette by plaiting sweet-smelling flowers into her hair and sweetening her breath with cloves.

Thus adorned, she proceeded to the pavilion where the maharaja awaited her. Enchanted by her beauty, the ruler pulled the courtesan toward him and asked her to share his cup of wine. She sipped the wine seductively; then, from a ring, the only ornament not given to her by her captor, she poured powdered poison into his cup and pressed the cup to his lips.

[10.] A HINDU GIRL DANCING. DECCAN, HYDERABAD, LATE 1600S.

DETAIL OF PL. [11]

DETAIL OF PL. [11]

[11.] CELEBRATION OF THE NEW YEAR AT THE COURT OF SHAH JAHAN. MUGHAL, CA. 1645.

The night of the most beautiful full moon comes after the season of rains and augers the New Year. On this night the ladies of the harem arrange a nocturnal entertainment for the sovereign. The ruler is seated on his dais, and the red earth around the pavilion is scattered with mica, glinting in the moonlight. In the lush gardens beyond, fountains splash colored water, and the fragrance of night flowers fills the air. A dancing-girl bows low to the ruler before striking the first pose of the kathak dance, the stance of a statue. As though touched by life under the ruler's gaze, she starts the opening movements of the dance. Her eyebrows arch, the long eyes move, then waist and torso undulate. Finally the feet, tied with anklets made of five hundred tiny bells, describe the intricate rhythms and patterns of the kathak.

Of all the great Indian dance forms, kathak demands mastery of the most elaborate rhythms, and the dancer's control of her feet must be total. In bravura passages of the performance, the dancer modulates her steps until the sound of her anklets descends from the clash of five hundred bells to the clear echo of a single bell. The dazzling display of footwork by the great exponents of kathak was reputed to have sent those who watched into a hypnotic trance.

When the lengthy ceremonies of a royal Indian wedding were over, the bridegroom assembled all the symbols of his power—his soldiers, his elephants, his horses, and his sword—to guard the person of a stranger, his new bride. Accompanied by her brother, the young bride, often little more than a child, was taken to the *doli,* or wedding palanquin, which would carry her away from all that was familiar and dear, to a land from which she could never return. As she began that fateful walk to her palanquin, the bride blessed the childhood home she was leaving by throwing rose petals and grains of rice over her shoulders, although cruel custom forbade her to look back at her family one last time. The poignancy of the departure was heightened by the wailing of reed instruments from the gateways of the bride's house, their keening notes perfectly expressing the desolation of the bride and the sorrow of her family. When the weeping bride finally left her brother's embrace to step into her wedding palanquin, surrounded by the vast entourage of her new husband, a solitary voice sang her grief:

"O my brother, they are taking me away! They are taking me away!
O my brother, what awaits me in a country of strangers?"

(illustration on following page)

DETAIL OF PL. [12]

[12.] WEDDING PROCESSION. MUGHAL, PATNA, CA. 1765.

[13.] HOLI FESTIVAL. MUGHAL, OUDH, CA. 1765.

Holi, the most unrestrained and colorful of India's religious festivals, occurs on the day of the summer equinox. In this season of flowers the presiding deity of the festival is often Kama, God of Pleasure. Like Cupid, Kama carries a bow, but Kama's bow is made of sugarcane. The bowstring is a line of humming bees, and Kama's arrows are flowers tipped with passion. In other parts of India, Holi celebrates the destruction of the she-demon Holika by the infant Lord Krishna.

Older than its own legends, the Holi festival is believed to have originated in ancient fertility rites, which are still celebrated with bacchanalian abandon. People recklessly smear one another with handfuls of colored powder made from crushed flowers until the sky is bright with the reds and pinks and ochers and purples of thrown powders.

DETAIL OF PL. [13]

Musk water mixed with colors is poured into long bamboo syringes, enabling men, women, and children to squirt one another with scented paints until everyone is splashed in vivid hues. In this melee the songs and dances of Holi are performed with an exuberant energy fueled by the Holi sweetmeats, which may be laced with opium and hashish.

Although a Hindu festival, even at the height of the Mughal Empire Holi was celebrated by people of all religions. During Holi the formality between men and women was suspended, and many liberties occurred that would not have been permitted on any other day of the year. Caste barriers disappeared. Monarch and subject smeared color on each other as equals, and for the brief span of a day the beggar played with the king.

Purdah gave a special poetry to Indian architecture. The desire to conceal women from view produced the inner courtyards, the verandahs, the intricate lattices and shutters of that private world. It was a domain unto itself, and some harem festivities were of a heart-stopping beauty. On the Night of the Full Moon in the pure white Pritam Niwas court-yard of Jaipur's City Palace there was dancing. All the women wore pink. There was absolute silence, no lights, only the moonlight washing the walls and glinting off their jewelry and gossamer veils.

The fulfillment of every sense was considered an art in the Indian courts. The blending of scents and perfumes and the discovery of the legendary attar of roses is credited to the Mughal Empress Nur Jahan. This elegant and beautiful Empress always bathed in a marble pool filled with the petals of a thousand roses. It is said that one evening when she was in her bath she noticed an oil-like substance floating on the water and, lowering her head, was intoxicated by the heady essence of roses. She commanded the oil to be collected and the precious fragrance—always compounded from a thousand roses—became the most sought-after perfume in India.

Scents were blended to suit mood and season and were believed to complement the color of clothing. In the summer heat the green scents of vetiver and lemon and other light fragrances such as sandalwood were worn with gossamer garments dyed in the palest hues. The spicy fragrances of musk and attar of roses and patchouli were used with the rich colors of winter silks. Dyers and washerwomen daubed freshly laundered cloth-ing with the preferred scents of the owner, and sticks of incense were burned in ward-robes to retain the scent.

Since the Indian garden was best enjoyed after sunset, when the heat of the day had passed, the harem gardens were planted with flowers to perfume the night. Frangipani, jasmine, queen of the night, and narcissi flourished between pleasure pavilions and lotus pools, their perfume heightened by the fragrances worn by the ladies of the harem. And on a terrace sat the begum queen of the harem, tranquilly smoking her hookah as she watched a dancer agilely balance flasks of perfume, while waves of the scents contained in the fragile glass bottles already wafted from gardens and attendants and garments, filling the night with fragrance.

[14.] ENTERTAINMENT IN A HAREM GARDEN. MUGHAL, FAIZABAD, CA. 1765.

DETAIL OF PL. [14]

[15.] SENIOR WIVES WITH AN ELDERLY EUNUCH PLAYING CHAUPAR IN THE COURT ZENANA . MUGHAL, LUCKNOW, CA. 1790.

The harem was a city of women. Its upper echelons consisted of the royal queens and princesses of the blood whose lives followed the same rigid etiquette as the ruler's court. Each queen had her own harem, her own *masnad,* or throne, her own cooks, reception rooms, and halls. She might not see her husband even once a month, yet she was still a wife and queen. The chief eunuch, a man of great influence, was the principal attendant of the king's first wife, the Padshah Begum.

Some of these queens or begums were, by dowry, enormously wealthy in their own right and wielded much power over their reigning husband or son. They intrigued, conducted business, and opposed the British from within the harem, or *zenana,* maintained personal armies, and rode in a covered palanquin with their own fabulously ornamented retinue in the great religious processions.

But the vast majority of harem women were ladies-in-waiting, maidservants, or concubines. These women generally entered the harem gates as children and spent their entire lives within its walls, unable to leave until they died. Many had never seen a garden or a river, a grove of trees or an open field.

Having neither the great positions nor the powerful ambitions of the royal ladies and condemned to a life of leisure and enforced companionship, these lesser harem women often treated one another with the deep affection of sisters. In select groups they strolled through the purdah gardens. They ate endless sweets and gossiped near the refreshing spray of colored fountains or admired their own reflections in lotus ponds. They laughed and shooed away the monkeys who swung and scampered down to steal a glittering trinket. In the evening, they sat in painted courtyards to play a game of *shatranj,* or Indian chess, moving jeweled pieces across an ivory and ebony board. Or they promenaded past the harem aviary, sighing as they compared their own existence to that of the caged birds.

[16.] COURTESAN AFTER BATHING. MUGHAL, DELHI, CA. 1815.

[17.] (LEFT) THE COURTESAN WHO LOVED CATS. MUGHAL, LUCKNOW, CA. 1835.

[18.] (RIGHT) A COURTESAN READY FOR VISITORS. MUGHAL, LUCKNOW, CA. 1835.

By the nineteenth century the court of the kingdom of Oudh had become so notorious for its decadence and stifling artifice that it was known as "The Orchid House." William Knighton, an Englishman in the service of King Nussir-ud-din of Oudh, has chronicled its excesses: the king's absolute power of life and death over his subjects, his lust for watching wild beasts tear each other to pieces in bloody combats as he sipped iced claret and nibbled biscuits, and his harem so unwieldy it had to be guarded by a regiment of women with muskets and bayonets.

He describes another class of harem attendants, the female bearers who carried the palanquins of the king and his ladies into the inner courts. Their chief, "a great masculine woman of pleasing countenance, was the poisoner of Nussir; bribed thereto by some member of the royal family."

Through his eyes we see the Padshah Begum's procession to a mosque to pray for "the greatest of all blessings . . . a male child." Only she could be preceded by kettle-drums (dunka), symbols of sovereignty, along with the embroidered umbrella, the sun symbol (aftadah), and the peacock feather fans. First came the king's bodyguard in blue and silver, band playing and colors unfurled. Then two battalions of infantry with bands and colors, a company of spearmen with silvered lances, the flag-bearers each with a royal emblazoned crimson banner. Then the Padshah Begum herself in a covered conveyance that "is in fact a small silver room borne on poles" supported by twenty bearers "dressed in white with scarlet turbans and loose scarlet overcoats edged with gold." The bearers are changed every quarter mile. The women bearers come next, then "the gold and silver sticks-in-waiting chanting the name and titles of the lady within." Behind them on his elephant rides the chief eunuch in turban and cloth of gold with rich cashmere shawls. A host of covered conveyances followed the eunuch, containing the two hundred ladies of the Padshah Begum's court. "You ask, what do they all do? The answer is, they do all sorts of things. Some of them are professed story-tellers in more senses than one. They lull their mistresses to sleep with tales after the manner of the *Arabian Nights.* Others shampoo well and are so employed for hours every day. Others sew. . . . Others read the Koran, the blue-stockings of the harem.

"So attended, with such crowds of followers and noisemakers, of both sexes and none, goes the Padshah Begum . . . thinking no little of her own greatness and of the noise her greatness makes in the world."

[19.] SOME OF THE KING'S WOMEN. MUGHAL, LUCKNOW, CA. 1815.

DETAIL OF PL. [19]

[20.] A NAWAB FROM LUCKNOW. MUGHAL, DELHI, 1852.

[21.] AN ELEGANT PAINTER FROM JAIPUR. MUGHAL, 1869.

[22.] PALANQUIN CARRIED BY RED-COATED BEARERS. BRITISH PERIOD, PATNA, MID-1800S.

[23.] KAISERBAGH PALACE. MUGHAL, LUCKNOW, MID-1800S.

DETAIL OF PL. 23

The Maharana of Udaipur was the premier king of the Rajput rulers, observing his religious duties with the extreme care necessary for a king who also carried the proud title "Sun of the Hindus." In time of peace the maharana arose before dawn and performed his ritual ablutions. Wrapping his body in a length of unstitched fabric known as the *dhoti,* he left his apartments for his private temple, which stood by water, as stipulated by the sacred texts. Gold and silver lamps lit the interior of the temple, and incense and camphor already burned before the deities. As the maharana entered the temple a conch shell was blown and the temple bells were rung to announce the commencement of the ruler's morning prayers.

The maharana seated himself before his Isht Devta, or personal godhead. Turmeric was smeared on the deity's forehead and garlands of marigolds hung around its neck. Between the fingers of his right hand the maharana held a rosary made of *rudraksh,* or forest seed beads, hidden in a *gomukhi,* or prayer gauntlet. The prayer gauntlet prevented the rosary, or *mala,* from being contaminated by the evil eye. The maharana recited the holy words of his mantra, or incantation, silently, as the text was too sacred to be spoken aloud. By the time the maharana had completed his lengthy sequence of prayers and meditations it was dawn, and the first reflections of the rising sun could be seen in the water outside the temple. The maharana ended his devotions by facing the rising sun with the words of the ancient Aryan prayer:

> "Thou that rise and are eternal,
> That ride in a chariot drawn by seven steeds,
> Your hair on fire and golden pendants in your ears,
> Thou Remover of darkness and evil,
> I worship thee."

[24.] RANA AMAR SINGH II (RULED 1698–1710) AT PRAYER. RAJPUT, MEWAR, CA. 1698.

[25.] RAO JAGAT SINGH OF KOTAH (RULED 1658–1670) IN HIS GARDEN. RAJPUT, KOTAH, CA. 1670.

The light garment worn by a princess over her apparel was known as the *peshwaz.* Although its purpose ostensibly was to veil, its effect was erotic rather than concealing. Only the most superior white muslins were used to make a *peshwaz,* and they were called by such poetic names as the white of the clouds when the rain is spent; the white of the August moon; the white of the conch shell; the white of the jasmine flower; the white of the sea surf. Finest of all was *shabnam,* the muslin of the morning dew. Yards and yards of this muslin were laid out on the palace lawns at dawn. If the muslin was so transparent that the royal ladies of the kingdom thought it was the dew, then at last a *peshwaz* could be made for a princess.

[26.] PRINCESS ADMIRING A BIRD. PUNJAB HILLS, CA. 1675.

[27.] RAJA JAI SINGH OF SAWAR WITH FEMALE MUSICIANS. RAJPUT, AJMER AREA, CA. 1690.

[28.] PRINCE AND LADIES SHOOTING HERON FROM A TERRACE. RAJPUT, BIKANER, CA. 1710.

[29.] TODI RAGINI. RAJPUT, KOTAH, CA. 1700.

In the great fort of Gwalior there can still be seen the ruins of a water duct once used to pipe water from the clear springs of the jungle into the forbidding citadel. The duct was built by Raja Man Singh of Gwalior so that his wife, a lovely goatherd, could assuage her homesickness by drinking the waters of her native jungle. Before she became the queen of Gwalior, the goatherd, known as Mrig Naini, the doe-eyed one, had lived in the jungle. Each morning she had ushered in the dawn with the music of her stringed instrument, the vina, drawing animals from their lairs to listen to the songs she sang in her golden voice. Man Singh, the king of Gwalior, was hunting in the jungle one morning when he heard Mrig Naini's song. Like the animals of the forest, he followed the beautiful sound until he found her in a clearing, surrounded by birds and beasts, her vina resting on her knees as she sang. Raja Man Singh fell in love and took her as his wife.

Mrig Naini came to live with Raja Man Singh in the mighty Gwalior fortress, continuing to enchant her husband as she had once enchanted the creatures of the jungle. She inspired him to compose a musical composition for the vina, the instrument she played so magically, and the king called his still-popular composition *Gujjari Todi,* the raga of the doe-eyed goatherd.

(illustration on preceding page)

So fierce are the summers of India that to this day the custom survives of offering water cooled in earthen pitchers to the parched passerby. As the blazing summer bakes the earth, men and animals search for any shaded place that might afford some respite from the relentless sun.

In earlier times the houses of the great were shrouded in *chiqs,* or cane screens, which were lowered in front of archways and windows. Vetiver blinds were soaked continually with water so that the hot breeze blowing against them was cooled and scented by the time it entered the rooms. The heat so assaulted every sense that even color became painful; in the summer months floors were covered with white sheets on which lay languid patricians loosely garbed in muslin garments dyed in palest pastels. They sipped sherbets iced with snow brought from the Himalayas by barges that plied the great Indian rivers. The only sounds they could tolerate were the splashing of marble fountains in their courtyards and the tinkling of crystal chandeliers above their heads. Large cloth fans, or *punkahs,* hung like sails from the high ceilings, their cords pulled day and night by *punkah wallahs,* or fan-boys.

[30.] JYESHTHA: THE HOT MONTH. RAJPUT, BIKANER, CA. 1725.

[31.] RAMA HUNTING BY MOONLIGHT. RAJPUT, KOTAH, 1781.

RAJPUT PAINTING

Of all the many martial duties required of an Indian king, none was so pleasant as the hunt. Well-versed in the strict hunting laws of the *Arthashastra,* which prevented disturbance of animal life during the mating seasons, the king had to gain mastery of the lance, the spear, the dagger, the bow and arrow, and finally the gun. He also took a personal interest in the breeding of his hunting animals. Falcons were trained to hawk a wide variety of birds. Cheetahs, the fastest animals in the world, were bred to course their natural prey, deer, without killing. Elephants had to learn not to bolt when attacked by enemies such as the lion or the panther. A horse had to respond immediately to the touch of a rider's knees in the furious pursuit of a jinking and vicious wild boar. And when the tiger, the king of the Indian jungle, was hunted, rulers, courtiers, and peasants all participated in the sport. Villagers brought *khabar,* or news, of a dangerous tiger at large in the vicinity. If the country was one of lush vegetation the hunting party stalked the tiger on elephant-back. If the region was sparsely wooded the hunters waited for their quarry on wooden towers, or *machans,* built near water holes, while armies of beaters, sometimes the entire population of local villages, circled the jungle, beating their sticks against copper vessels to frighten the tiger toward the waiting weapons.

Another method required a platform to be built in the branches of a tree, where the hunters sat silently through the night watching for the tiger. An animal such as a goat or lamb with a bell tied around its neck was secured to the base of the tree as bait. The constant movement of the frightened animal set its bell ringing, and the hunters waited for the tiger to be lured into investigating this unnatural sound. It was considered a feat to kill a tiger before it could reach the bait. Hunters who managed to do so became the heroes of their adoring ladies for having saved the life of an innocent lamb.

DETAIL OF PL. 31

[32.] RAO RAM SINGH I OF KOTAH (RULED 1686–1708) CHASES A RHINOCEROS. RAJPUT, KOTAH, CA. 1695.

[33.] LION HUNT. RAJPUT, KISHANGARH, CA. 1735.

[34.] BY THE LIGHT OF THE MOON, LAMPS, AND FIREWORKS. RAJPUT, KISHANGARH, CA. 1740.

It was the ambition of every concubine to become the favorite of the *zenana* and ensure the maharaja's love. Using her maid as her accomplice, a concubine devoted most of her life toward achieving this dream. Hours of ennui were vanquished by mistress and servant as they plotted the seduction and enslavement of the maharaja. The maidservant assisted her mistress in voluptuous self-adornment, painting the concubine's nipples or spreading rouge in the hollow of her breasts to make her more desirable. When the concubine was feverish with desire the maid fanned her gently or spread a cooling paste of henna between her thighs to soothe her longing. Together mistress and maid poured over old texts containing erotic spells in observation of the *Kama Sutra*'s command:

> You must fetter his soul
> Before you bind your body to his in lovemaking.

They prepared potent aphrodisiacs from crushed rubies, peacock's bones, or the testicles of a ram and hid these in secret caskets, awaiting an opportunity to use them on the ruler. After consulting horoscopes, the concubine decided on an auspicious date for the seduction and sent her maidservant to scan the court calendar to discover which harem ceremonies required the maharaja's presence in the *zenana*. When the night finally came, the two women chose an appropriate arch in the maharaja's passageway. The concubine, clad in diaphanous garments, stood in the arch with her maidservant by her side, dressed at her dowdiest to enhance her mistress's beauty. The maharaja and his entourage passed. A few hours later, if the concubine's prayers were answered, the chief eunuch returned, his lamp held high, to summon the concubine to the *Preet Chatra,* or Love Pavilion.

(illustration on following page)

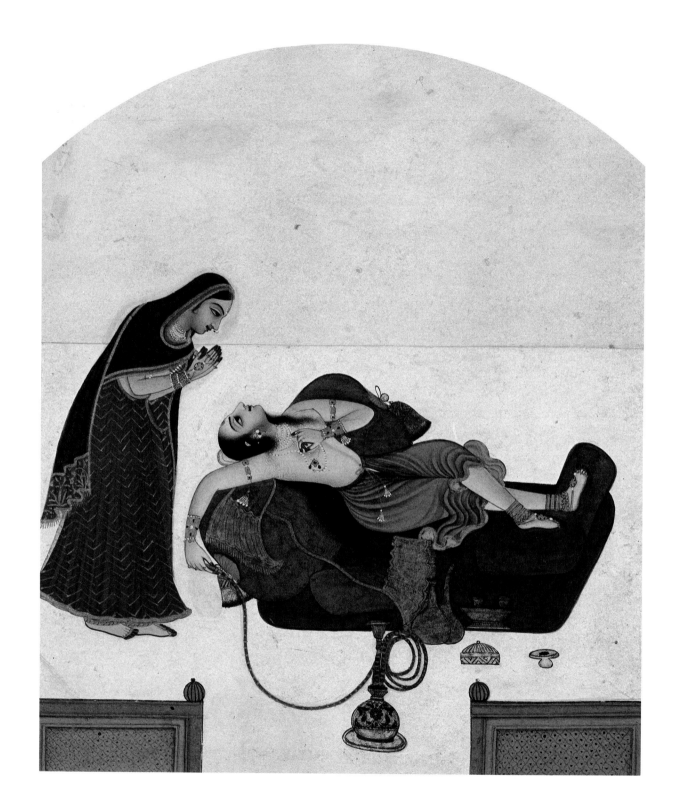

[35.] LONGING. RAJPUT, BUNDI, MID-1700S.

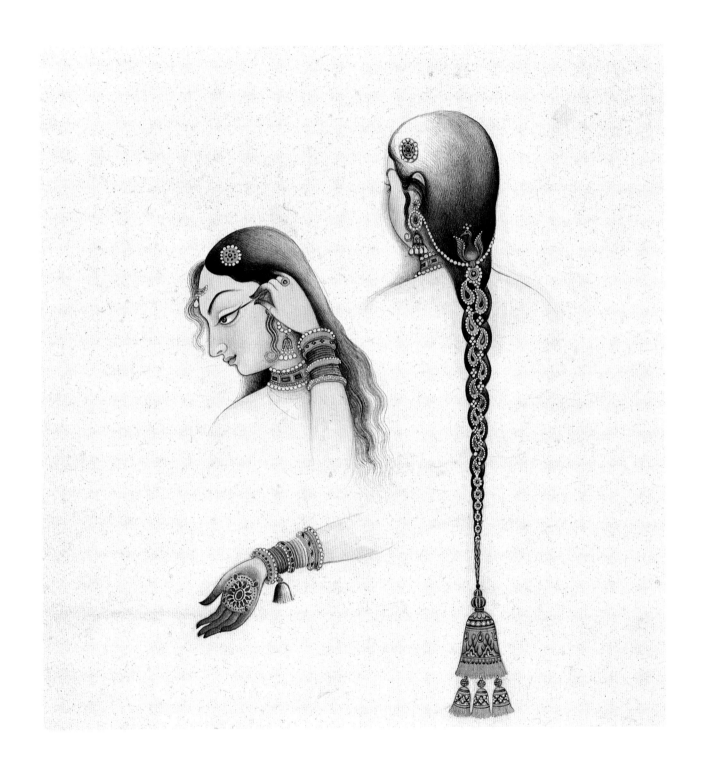

As summer singed the plains of Hindustan, the Great Mughal Jahangir commenced his imperial progress to the Vale of Kashmir, at the feet of the Himalayas. Kashmir's shining lakes and mountain peaks provided an idyllic site for an Emperor's repose. Here Jahangir —an enthusiastic naturalist—surveyed the beauties and curiosities of nature at his leisure, dictating his observations to scribes for his imperial memoirs, the *Tuzuk-i-Jahangiri.* Around him, harem ladies, invigorated by the mountain air, lay on dhurries, or cloth carpets, spread under the shade of huge plane trees, planning frivolous entertainments while their more accomplished colleagues composed clever couplets for his diversion. *Kanats,* or cloth screens, preserved the privacy of his court from the vulgar gaze.

Riding past fields of saffron near the village of Vernag, the Emperor once chanced upon a clear pool filled with large fish. He gave instructions that gold rings be put through the noses of some of them to amuse the Empress. The pool became a favorite pleasure spot for Jahangir's court, and the Empress took great delight in watching the ornamented fish shimmer through the clear water. Forty years later, the French traveler François Bernier visited Kashmir and the pool at Vernag. His diary records that the larger fish still wore their royal decorations.

[36.] LOVERS STROLLING BY A POOL. PUNJAB HILLS, KANGRA, CA. 1780.

[37.] LADY PLAYING A TANPURA. PUNJAB HILLS, CA. 1780.

[38.] BABY WORSHIP: A FAMILY AT PLAY. PUNJAB HILLS, EARLY 1800S.

The six primary Indian musical compositions, the ragas, celebrate the seasons. Of all the seasons, none inspires more music than the monsoon. Torrential rains bathe an earth scorched by the searing heat of summer. Dying foliage becomes lush again. Animals and birds begin their courting. The season is symbolized in Indian painting by the lyrical image of a peacock, its brilliant feathers fully fanned, dancing in the rain.

The privileged took their leisure in marble wind pavilions open to the cool breezes of the season, and orchestras of singers and musicians sang the *Raga Megh,* the raga of the rains, as they were exhorted to do by the poet Ghalib, who wrote:

> Be festive, mortals.
> The sky is girdled with stars,
> The earth garlanded with flowers.
> Nature has decorated herself to seduce you
> In the season of rains.

[39.] THE MONTH OF RAIN. PUNJAB HILLS, KANGRA, CA. 1810.

[40.] A DAY AT GAGRAUN FORT. RAJPUT, KOTAH, CA. 1735.

[41.] DURBAR HALL. UNIDENTIFIED MARATHA SCHOOL, CA. 1820.

The durbar hall was the hall of royal audience, and when the king gave audience he was known as the Durbar. All the notables of the kingdom attended a state durbar. Seated on either side of the ruler according to status, they guarded their precedence and prerogatives jealously, since such an audience publicly revealed a noble's significance in the eyes of the ruler, informing the kingdom of his current prestige and power. Also present were the spiritual leader of the kingdom, the important ministers who controlled the country's finances and administration, and the commander of the nation's armed forces.

Some Indian rulers took the precaution of having priests cast astrological charts for an important durbar, to ensure harmony among their ambitious nobles and preserve balance in the country's political life. These charts drew their inspiration from the balance of the celestial spheres, and in their astrological placements the priests tried to recreate the universe in microcosm. The king was the sun. The nobles were the planets. Lesser personages represented minor heavenly bodies. The whole audience was designed to remind those present that the king was the center of their galaxy and any threat to his position would disturb the proper functioning of the entire kingdom.

(illustration on preceding page)

The Mughal emperors were famous for their love of flowers, in particular the rose, which they introduced to India. Motifs of roses and many other flowers appear in profusion in Mughal monuments such as the Taj Mahal. Later kings, whether Muslim or Hindu, popularized these Mughal flowers in their own schools of art. Flowers were embroidered on clothes. They were woven into precious carpets and cloth hangings. They were painted and printed on ceremonial tents. Marble walls were inlaid with floral designs of semiprecious stones such as lapis lazuli, cornelian, and malachite, and even great gems were carved in the shapes of flowers.

In the portraits of this period a king is often shown gazing at a flower held in his hand. The image has two meanings. It shows the ruler as a lover of beauty and a patron of the arts. More significantly, the king, who is himself the flower of his people's aspirations, gazes at a perfect blossom with the same admiration that is in his subjects' eyes when they gaze upon him.

[42.] MARAJA MAN SINGH OF JODHPUR (RULED 1804–1843) SNIFFS A PINK. RAJPUT, MARWAR, EARLY 1800S.

The boast of the marauding Afghans who swept down from their mountains to raid the fertile Punjab plains of northern India was that "the grass never grows where their horses have once trodden." But at the end of the eighteenth century the Afghans met their match in a young Sikh prince of the Punjab, Maharaja Ranjit Singh. Maharaja Ranjit Singh quelled the Afghan menace, and during the forty years of his reign he unified a war-torn Punjab, bringing calm out of chaos. By 1830 his dominions stretched from the borders of China to the river Sutlej. His subjects numbered seventy million people. Trade flourished. His capital city of Lahore became an important center for the caravan trains that plied the golden routes between Istanbul and Peking. Maharaja Ranjit Singh was a man of great modesty and tolerance, who never lost the common touch. People of all religions lived in peace within his territories. Unlike other monarchs, he did not have coins struck in his own name. As a devout Sikh he had his coins embossed with the Sikh gurus, and his coinage was known as the *Nanak Shahi (shahi* is a coin, and Nanak was the first apostle of the Sikhs.) A great warrior and a great king, Maharaja Ranjit Singh was known to his people as "The Lion of the Punjab," despite his unprepossessing physical stature, his pockmarked skin, and the fact that he had only one eye.

Although Ranjit Singh had not received an adequate education as a young man, he made up for this deficiency once he had brought peace to his dominions. In the latter years of his reign, The Lion of the Punjab satisfied his craving for knowledge by constantly badgering scholars, intellectuals, and visitors from distant lands with questions. He was avidly curious, keeping his one eye glued to his visitors as he assaulted them with an inexhaustible supply of questions from which they could not escape. "His conversation is like a nightmare," wrote one drained victim of Maharaja Ranjit Singh's interrogations, the Frenchman Jacquemont. "He has asked me a hundred thousand questions about India, the British, Europe, Bonaparte, this world in general and the next, hell, paradise, the soul, God, the devil, and a myriad others of the same kind."

[43.] A SIKH PRINCE AND TUTOR IN A PAVILION DURING THE MONSOON. PUNJAB, CA. 1835.

In India there are still stone slabs that denote historic battlefields, marking the spot where a warrior has fallen in combat. A horse with a halo above its head is carved on each slab, but the image of the warrior is absent. The reason for this curious omission is that in battle the warrior and his mount became a single weapon, and the horse is the symbol of their joint valor.

Perhaps the most legendary steed of a warrior king was the charger Chetak, who carried the Rajput king Rana Pratap into battle against a mighty army commanded by the son of the Mughal Emperor. A nineteenth-century Englishman, Colonel James Tod, paid homage to the valor of rider and horse in his description of this famous battle: ". . . the lance of the Rajput would have deprived Akbar of his heir. His steed, the gallant Chetak, nobly seconded his lord, and is represented . . . with one foot raised upon the elephant of the Moghul, while his rider has his lance propelled against his foe. . . ."

So close was the relationship between warrior and mount that the horse that carried a king was appareled like a king. On its head was an aigrette like the one that crowned the ruler's turban. Around its chest were massive necklaces of gold and precious stones; encircling its fetlocks were heavy anklets, marking the horse, like its master, a monarch.

[44.] PRITHVI SINGH OF KISHANGARH (RULED 1840–1880) RIDING WITH HIS SON. RAJPUT, KISHANGARH, 1841.

[45.] A BOY MAHARAJA OF INDORE IN DURBAR. CENTRAL INDIA, INDORE, CA. 1850.

As a symbol of the divine, on occasions of religious ceremony, the Hindu king is enshrined in a pavilion that resembles a miniature temple and is attended by a priest who fans him as though he were a deity. Paintings of such ceremonies show a sacred halo encircling the maharaja's head. Behind him is the forest at dusk, nature resting under the protection of the king. Half-visible trees bear fruit that is sacred to the Hindus and offered in their temple rites—the mango, the banana, the coconut—commemorating the place where the Lord Krishna once lived, Madhuban, the Forest of Honey.

By the nineteenth century, alien elements intrude on the idyl. Europe has stolen into the Forest of Honey. The god-king's throne is a French armchair. Between himself and Lord Krishna's sacred jungle lies a terrace made of Italian tiles where polite English roses grow discreetly in Victorian jardinieres. Although the young prince, like an idol, is still cocooned in the trappings of deity, the god-king's halo is now reflected in a gilt-framed Venetian mirror or lit by imported European chandeliers.

[46] BOY KING WITH BRAHMIN PRIEST. KOTAH, 1880.

[47.] THE MAHARAJA OF BHURTPORE (BHARATPUR) IN DURBAR. SHEPHERD AND ROBERTSON, CA. 1865.

[48.] SIR PRATAP SINGH WITH THE MAHARAJA SARDAR SINGH OF JODHPUR AS A CHILD.

[49.] H. H. SIR ANAND RAO PUAR, MAHARAJA OF DHAR WITH HIS NEPHEW, THE HEIR APPARENT. RAJA LALA DEEN DAYAL, CA. 1889.

[50.] H. H. MAHRAJ ADHIRA MADAN SINGH BAHADUR, MAHARAJA OF KISHANGARH. 1903.

[51.] THE MAHARAJA OF KHOLAPORE. BOURNE AND SHEPARD, CA. 1860S.

[52.] BARA IMAMBARA. SAMUEL BOURNE, LUCKNOW, 1860S.

[53.] COURTESAN OF LUCKNOW. CA. 1880.

Lucknow, the opulent capital of Oudh, was celebrated for its accomplished courtesans. These voluptuaries were patronized and favored by the kings, paid princely sums by merchants, and immortalized in romantic verse by poets. Moving through the streets of Lucknow in their curtained palanquins, they were pursued by lovesick gallants able to recognize the elusive objects of their desire from the invisible signature left in the air by their distinctive perfumes. At night, in their gilded establishments, the courtesans entertained their clients to the most refined music, dance, poetry, and lovemaking.

[54.] COURTESAN WITH ATTENDANT. CA. 1860S.

The beautiful courtesan was a woman a man could not possess as he did his wives and concubines, and the courtesans of Lucknow added that element of adventure to a man's life lacking in his crowded harem. By her exquisite manners the courtesan made each patron feel she entertained the tenderest feelings for him, yet no man could feel secure of her affections when he knew her behavior was equally tender to his rivals. Her clothing inspired desire. Revealing bodices were veiled in the finest gauzes and muslins. Jewelry suggestively cinched waists and bosoms. Diaphanous pantaloons and skirts fell in flamboyant flares, but were knotted at the waist with such intricacy that only the courtesan herself knew how to undo them.

These knotted silken cords sometimes came to a courtesan's assistance. Once a beautiful courtesan, the favorite of a king, was separated from her master in a battle. As she tried to rejoin him she was taken captive by a boorish enemy general. Paying no heed to the courtesan's frantic protests, the general took her into his tent and proceeded to molest her. He lustfully tore off her heavy jewelry and outer garments to find himself faced with the elaborate knots of her girdle. Before the general succeeded in finding the right tassel for the right cord, her patron's soldiers burst into the tent, killed her tormentor, and took her back to the king.

Courtesans also cast their spell on the English merchants and adventurers who amassed huge fortunes in India in the eighteenth century and who were starved of female companionship because their women were reluctant to join them in the debilitating climate. These nabobs, a bastardization of the word "nawab," meaning a Muslim prince, lived like Indian potentates, smoking from hookahs, reclining on bolsters, and taking local dancing-girls and courtesans as their mistresses. Often these couples became devoted to each other. The diarist William Hickey's beloved Jemdanee was "as gentle and affectionately attached a girl as ever a man was blessed with."

The girl in Plate 55 wears a portrait of her patron, the maharaja. Probably of a very simple background, she must have been awed by every moment spent outside her limited world. Yet if she was sufficiently appealing, quick, and ambitious, she might have been taken all the way to London or Paris, the outer limits of her prince's new playground.

कलमगीपीलाजीमसतरकी

[55.] A MUSLIM COURTESAN. RAJPUT, MARWAR, JODHPUR, CA. 1875.

[56.] COURTESAN OF LUCKNOW. CA. 1880.

There was never a time when intoxicants were not used in India. Ash-covered mystics, obsessed with altered states of mind, used drugs to open the doors of perception. Drugs and spirits were given to warriors before a battle to inflame their courage so they became oblivious to the dangers of combat. In the sybaritic courts of India, intoxicants were the natural complement of leisure, and endless poems and songs drew lyrical parallels between the madness of love and the headiness of inebriation.

There were as many courtly intoxicants as modes of courtship. Elaborate hubble-bubbles, or hookahs, were used to inhale scented tobacco blended with hashish. Precious gems—rubies, emeralds, pearls—were crushed into wines. From elegant vessels inlaid with silver and gold these spirits were poured by *sakhis,* or maids, who carried the wine. Circular ivory boxes painted with poppy flowers held opium. And no meeting or farewell was complete without sweetening the mouth with an offering of *paan* (slices of betel nut mixed with lime wrapped in the leaf of the betel pepper) from its intricate casket.

[57.] DANCING GIRL, JEYPORE (JAIPUR). CA. 1885.

[58.] "SIRDARS" (NOBLEMEN). SHEPHERD AND ROBERTSON.

[59.] MAHARAO UMED SINGH OF KOTAH. CA. 1885.

[60.] "THE SPANISH MAHARANI." MAHARANI ANITA DELGRADA OF KAPURTHALA. RAJA LALA DEEN DAYAL, AUGUST 1914.

[61.] MUSLIM COURT, HYDERABAD. RAJA LALA DEEN DAYAL.

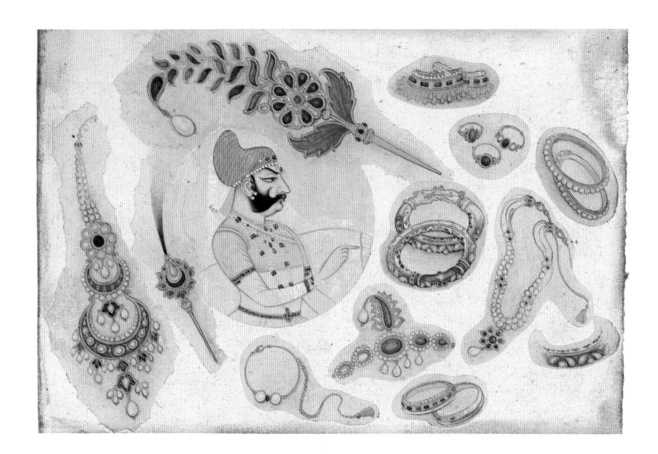

India was famed for its fabulous jewels. The mines of Golconda yielded incomparable diamonds. Tonk was known for its emeralds. The best sapphires were mined in Kashmir, the best rubies in Burma, and divers extracted unparalleled pearls from the Persian Gulf.

In Indian astrology, precious stones were thought to represent the planets. A ruby was a manifestation of the sun and its energy. A sapphire denoted Saturn and its restraining influence. Gems were worn both as ornamentation and to invite the auspicious aura of the planets they symbolized.

It was said of the greatest Indian diamond, the Koh-i-noor, that it influenced destiny by never remaining overlong in the hands of its possessors. At one time the Koh-i-noor belonged to the frivolous Mughal Emperor Mohammed Shah. When forced to treat with his Persian conqueror, Nadir Shah, the Mughal Emperor cunningly concealed the Koh-i-noor in the folds of his turban. The wily Persian insisted on exchanging turbans as a mark of friendship, thus making off with India's most precious jewel.

[62.] SOUTH INDIAN MAHARAJA.

[63.] (OPPOSITE) THE BEGUM OF BHOPAL WITH ATTENDANTS. CA. 1860S.

[64.] (ABOVE) "HINDOO LADIES." CA. 1900.

[65.] THE MAHARAO RAJA RAGHUBIR SINGH BAHADUR OF BUNDI. CA. 1890.

[66.] INTERIOR OF GWALIOR PALACE. RAJA LALA DEEN DAYAL, CA. 1880.

[67.] MAHARAJA SINDIA OF GWALIOR AND SUITE. BOURNE AND SHEPARD. 1877.

[68.] TWO MAHARAJAS OF RAJASTHAN. UNIDENTIFIED SCHOOL, CA. 1865.

[69.] H. H. SIR SHER MAHOMED KHAN, G.D.I.E., DIVAN OF PALANPUR. 1903.

Courtly turbans consisted of yards of fabric, often more than twenty feet long, which were wound into astonishing shapes and decorated with jeweled aigrettes, pendants, or a crownlike ornament called the *sarpej.* The style of a turban identified a person's region and, more importantly, his prestige and power.

Apart from indicating grandeur and origin the turban had its practical uses. On a journey the turban protected the traveler from the scorching rays of the sun, serving as a shield against sand or dust. At night it became an agreeable pillow for his head. The thirsty traveler tied a water vessel to one end of his turban: the vast length of cloth enabled him to lower the vessel into deep wells. In combat a turban cushioned the head from fatal blows. A warrior bound his injuries with strips torn from his turban or disguised himself by using the end of his turban to mask his face. The ultimate gesture of humiliation for a defeated warrior was the act of laying his turban at the feet of his victor.

[70.] PRINCELY OFFICERS FROM MALWA. RAJA LALA DEEN DAYAL.

[71.] THE MAHARAJA OF PANNA. CA. 1885.

[72.] A SIKH RULER, PERHAPS THE MAHARAJA OF PATIALA. PUNJAB, CA. 1885.

[73.] H. H. SHRI SIR MANSINGHJI SOORSINGHJI, K.D.S.I., THAKORE SAHEB OF PALITANA. 1903.

The footwear of the principal people of the land distinguished them from mere pedestrians. Like a line of jeweled objects, slippers would be seen abandoned outside great entrances while their owners reclined on bolstered cushions within. Embroidered in gold and silver thread, they were the final signature to the gorgeous apparel of a courtier. Sometimes they occasioned poetic gestures. A string of pearls was used to measure a princess's foot for her slipper, and the excess pearls were thrown as largesse to her maids. Great nobles, tiring of the attentions of their courtesans, subtly informed them of the end of a liaison with the gift of a pair of exquisite slippers pointed in the direction of the gate.

Sometimes they were the subject of history. In the middle of the nineteenth century a placid nawab found himself reluctantly embroiled in momentous events. While British troops combed rebellious Oudh, the nawab called for his attendants and other hangers-on, only to hear his own voice echoing in his empty palace. His melancholic isolation was remedied when British soldiers burst into his chamber and took him captive. Flung into a crowded dungeon, the nawab was surrounded by his more courageous contemporaries, who were shocked by his uncharacteristic valor. When questioned, the nawab explained, "Why I too would have run away had there been anyone to aid me with my slippers."

[74.] (LEFT) NAWAB ASAF-UD-DAULAH OF OUDH (RULED 1775–1797). BENGAL, CALCUTTA, CA. 1826.

[75.] (RIGHT) NADIR SHAH OF THE AFSHARID DYNASTY OF PERSIA (RULED 1736–1747). BENGAL, CALCUTTA, CA. 1826.

[76.] THE NAWAB OF CHAWNEPORE (KANPUR). BOURNE AND SHEPARD, CA. 1870S.

[77.] PALACE OF RAUSHAN-UD-DAULAH. LUCKNOW, CA. 1870; SAMUEL BOURNE, ENGLISH, B. 1834–D. 1912.

[78.] TIPOO SULTAN'S PALACE IN BANGALORE.

[79.] INTERIOR OF DIWAN-I-KHASS. SAMUEL BOURNE, DELHI, 1860S.

[80.] THE NEPHEW OF THE LAST KING OF DELHI AND HIS SONS. SHEPHERD AND ROBERTSON, CA. 1865.

[81.] (ABOVE) THE LAST MUGHAL EMPEROR, BAHADUR SHAH II, WITH TWO SONS. MUGHAL, 1838.

[82.] (OPPOSITE) BAHADUR SHAH II IN EXILE. ATTRIBUTED TO P. H. EGERTON, CA. 1858.

Once the principal seat of a great empire before which all India had trembled, in Bahadur Shah II's reign the Red Fort lay sad and neglected, its delicate plasterwork peeling, its arches shrouded in cobwebs. In the 1830s Emily Eden, sister of Lord Auckland, the British Governor-General of India, visited the Red Fort. She wrote of crumbling pavilions, their jeweled inlays long stolen and marble baths filled with disheveled guards, observing that "Delhi is a very suggestive and moralising place. Such stupendous remains of power passed and passing away." In a garden she came upon the solitary figure of the old Emperor himself. A lone attendant whisked flies from the pages of his book.

The last of the Mughal emperors, whose writ ran no further than the battlements of his Red Fort in Delhi, may have been impoverished and powerless, but Bahadur Shah was a renowned patron of the arts, and his dwindling court retained its refined manners and etiquette. A gifted poet, the Emperor's own poems record his changed circumstances with greater poignancy than Emily Eden.

> All that I loved is gone
> Like a garden robbed of its beauty by autumn,
> I am only a memory of splendour.

[83.] INTERIOR OF THE TOMB OF ETAHMADOLAH (ITIMAD-UD-DAULAH). BRITISH PERIOD, CA. 1815.

Epilogue

For many centuries Indian rulers resided in palace-forts situated in the heart of their capital cities. Living in such accessible proximity to their people, the kings were acutely conscious of their subjects' desires and grievances, and the subjects responded to this concern by giving the ruler the affectionate title *ma-baap,* meaning parent.

In the nineteenth century, when the policy of paramountcy had extended British influence over the whole of princely India, the British encouraged Indian rulers to build inaccessible palaces outside the royal capitals in a deliberate attempt to divorce the ruler from his people and strengthen their own influence. The ruler had little option but to accommodate the British. His power no longer came from the approval of his people; it emanated from the approval of the British Raj. Indian rulers who fought against British encroachment on their kingdoms were swiftly forced into exile or made to abdicate. As one British historian stated categorically, "The whisper of the British resident is command to the Indian king."

The new palaces mushrooming all over royal India in the nineteenth century were built in a wide variety of hy-

"The Big Guns"

States with of 15 Guns
Salutes or More

The 21-Gun States	Kotah
Hyderabad	Patiala
Gwalior	Bahawalpur
Mysore	Cochin
Kashmir	Rewa
Baroda	
	The 15-Gun States
The 19-Gun States	Sikkim
Travancore	Sirohi
Bhopal	Jaisalmer
Kolhapur	Banswara
Indore	Dungapur
Udaipur	Partabgarh
Kalat	Alwar
	Kishengarh
The 17-Gun States	Dholpur
Cutch	Khairpur
Bikaner	Dhar
Jodhpur	Datia
Jaipur	Dewas (Junior)
Tonk	Dewas (Senior)
Bharatpur	Idar
Bundi	Orchha
Karauli	Bhutan

brid styles. Given such sonorous architectural names as Indo-Saracenic and Renaissance Oriental, they were stuffed with Victorian or Edwardian artifacts and furniture. Their isolated maharajas no longer used durbar halls to dispense justice. Instead, the rulers and nobles of mighty kingdoms became caricatures of oriental splendor in durbar halls designed to impress the maharajas' new overlords —the British. The durbar halls acquired another, and for India, entirely original, function: they now doubled as ballrooms. The palaces also contained other essentials for British recreation—billiard rooms, tennis courts, cricket pitches—and the perfumed lotus baths of India were replaced by the diving board and the swimming pool.

Instead of earning accolades such as *ma-baap* from their people, the emasculated Indian princes now fought for the new titles being scattered like confetti over royal India by the British Empire. Knighthoods and orders such as The Star of India and The Order of the Indian Empire helped disguise the humiliations of lost power, although the most important weapon held by the British over the *amour propre* of an Indian ruler was the gun salute. The number of gun salutes fired for an Indian ruler established his significance, and the British exercised a subtle control on princely India by increasing or decreasing the amount of a ruler's salutes to indicate their pleasure. In slavish imitation of Europe, Indian rulers also began adopting coats of arms, sometimes even commissioning Latin mottoes to describe their ancestry. Only a closer look at the quarterings revealed the presence of India in the shape of an elephant *rampant* or a coiled serpent.

But the British themselves had been seduced by the splendor and leisure of the Indian courts. In his magnificent Viceregal Palace in Calcutta and later in Delhi, the British Viceroy held his own durbars with a pomp that rivaled the durbars of the Great Mughals. One British Viceroy, suffused with imperial hauteur, is said to have remarked, "The Emperor of China and I rule half the world and still have time for breakfast."

Attending the viceregal durbars as virtual vassals, the Indian rulers, garbed in magnificent robes and jewels, circulated under huge chandeliers and oil paintings like brilliantly plumaged birds. Yet their long tunic coats were no longer made solely from Indian brocades and silks, but from Shanghai satins, Lyons wools, and Italian velvets. Instead of elaborate slippers encrusted with gems, their feet were now shod in satin pumps with bows—*de rigeur* footwear for formal viceregal gatherings. Impressive epaulettes had also arrived on royal Indian shoulders, but in the journey had gained an Indian touch and were now fashioned from pearls.

When they retired to their harems, the rulers reverted to the traditional costumes of their courts, a manner of dress that had never been abandoned by their ladies. The Muslim begum still wore her flared pantaloons and the Hindu maharani her elaborate sari, although the Edwardian era had crept into their chemises, with the hint of the flounce and the ruffle, and into the alcoves of their chambers, where imported nude statuettes swooned with desire or warped in the heat.

Back in their own apartments, the Indian princes were busy installing vast Western-style dressing rooms to accommodate their newly acquired Western clothes. The largest of these wardrobes belonged to the sixth Nizam of Hyderabad, Mahbub Ali Khan. It filled an entire wing of his

Fig. 4. *Khansamas: The Wardrobe Attendants of the Nawabs of Rampur. 1930.*

These retainers, who intermarried and whose functions were hereditary, were completely trusted by the family and held the keys to various treasure chambers.

The *Tokshakhana:* separate chambers for men's and women's valuable clothing and bolts of uncut textiles.

The *Jawarkhana:* for family jewels and religious items studded with precious stones.

The *Aabdarkhana:* for storable food and water. Jade "poison plates" were kept here, and water sealed in silver vessels. Thirty people were employed to taste the food and water at random. The Rampur nawabs also employed eighty chefs, each of whom excelled in a particular dish.

The *Kawalkhana:* for chandeliers, candelabra, fans, decorative objects, crystal, Venetian glass, rose quartz, and jade.

The *Farashkhana:* for *masnads,* the elaborate floor coverings and cushions for royalty to sit on. For tentage, dhurries, carpets, and the magnificent embroidered silk and velvet tents used for the Muslim festival of Muharram.

The young boy second from right is now fifty-five years old, still in the employ of the family.

palace and stood two stories high. Made of Burma teak, it resembled a cloister more than a cupboard. Two hand-managed lifts brought down life-sized dummies appareled in garments the Nizam might be tempted to wear, although the fastidious Mahbub Ali Khan is reputed never to have worn a garment twice.

And what happened to the heir to an Indian kingdom in this confused era? Obviously the traditional education imparted by the kingdom's gurus was no longer adequate. New boarding schools were founded by the British to teach the scions of Indian royal houses how to recite Shakespeare and how to play cricket. These establishments were sometimes referred to as the "Etons of the East"—though the masters of the original Eton might have looked askance at the retinues of their new pupils, who arrived for the first day of school with their elephants, their horses, their soldiers, and their child-brides.

One of the first Indian princes to be molded by the British was Maharaja Duleep Singh of Punjab, son of Maharaja Ranjit Singh, the great king who had been called by his people "The Lion of Punjab." During the young prince's childhood the British annexed his territories and packed him off to exile in England. Queen Victoria took a maternal interest in the handsome young maharaja and even commissioned Franz Winterhalter to paint a portrait of Duleep Singh posing in Buckingham Palace. She herself did an occasional sketch of her protégé and was concerned about his indifference to the hazards of the English climate. The Empress of India frequently advised the stateless Indian maharaja to wear warm underclothing. Duleep Singh, accustomed to the luxurious fabrics of India, pleaded, "Indeed, Ma'am, I cannot bear the feel of flannel

E P I L O G U E

next to my skin. It makes me long to scratch and you would not like to see me scratching in your presence." Their relationship was somewhat soured by the fact that Duleep Singh had been robbed not just of his country but also of his great diamond, the Koh-i-noor, by Victoria's Empire, and the young maharaja was known to grumble in private, "She has no more right to that diamond than I have to Windsor Castle."

While dispossessed Indian princes were being sketched by British Empresses, the reigning Indian rulers were playing host to an army of royal European visitors—Princes of Wales, tsarevitches of Russia, archdukes from Austro-Hungary, the young German Crown Prince who was to dismantle Europe when he became kaiser, pretenders to the throne of France, all-powerful British viceroys, as well as legions of dukes and other lesser grandees. Social climbers angled avidly for invitations to these splendid gatherings, and if they succeeded they were entertained with a style and magnificence unmatched in the world. From breathtaking wedding ceremonies uniting favorite dogs in matrimony, to spectacular shoots, to grand balls, every minute of every day gave credence to the legend of princely Indian hospitality.

The soldier-statesman of the kingdom of Bikaner, Maharaja Ganga Singh, was famed for his annual sand grouse shoot. On these fabulous shoots there was a veritable massacre of the sand grouse, a little bird that makes delicious eating. But could the fourteen guns that bagged eleven thousand birds in one day possibly have consumed the fruit of their sport, no matter how delicious? Perhaps it was the sight of such slaughter that led one wag attending the maharaja's shoot to observe that Ganga Singh was Ma-

Maharaja Ranjit Singh, "The Lion of Punjab." Bannu.

Maharaja Duleep Singh. Winterhalter. Copyright reserved. Courtauld Institute of Art.

171

Fig. 5. *The Prince of Wales' First Tiger.*
Bourne and Shepard, ca. 1870.

Portrait of Maharaja Ganga Singh.

haraja of Bikaner only by the "grouse of God." Another wit, commenting on another kingdom's entertainment plans for a forthcoming visit by a Prince of Wales, composed this poem:

> Beautifully he will shoot
> Many a royal tiger brute.
> Lying on their backs they die
> Shot by the apple of their eye.

Sir Pratap Singh of Jodhpur, an excellent shot and even greater rider, was every Englishman's idea of the chivalrous Indian knight. Friend to Queen Victoria, Edward VII, George V, and three times Regent of the kingdom of Jodhpur during the minorities of three successive maharajas, Sir Pratap believed fervently in the martial traditions of the Rajput warrior. At the time of the Boxer Rebellion in China, Sir Pratap formed an impressive fighting force from the young nobles of Jodhpur to assist the British Empire. Splendidly uniformed in white and gold, the Jodhpur Lancers, together with other royal Indian cavalries such as the Gwalior Lancers, the Mysore Lancers, the Hyderabad Lancers, the Patiala Lancers, the Jaipur Lancers, and many more, acquitted themselves brilliantly in campaigns spanning the Boxer Rebellion of 1899 to the battlefields of World War II.

On his way to attend Queen Victoria's Golden Jubilee celebrations in London, Sir Pratap Singh of Jodhpur had the misfortune of losing all his luggage at sea. The grandeur of the occasion required an immediate replacement of his splendid clothes. In explaining the cut of his breeches to a London tailor, Sir Pratap inadvertently set the fashion for trousers that have borne his name ever since—jodhpurs. As puritanical as the Empress he loved, the Victorian Sir Pratap once refused to dance with a continental lady dressed in a décolleté gown because "I think she not a very gentlemanly lady." And he insisted that the ladies of his own harem wear long sleeves because he thought they looked immodest when they fanned themselves, although no man could see them but himself.

By the turn of the twentieth century the Indian rulers were mesmerized by the luxurious inventions of the West. They happily exchanged the ardors of traveling in caravans and sleeping in pitched tents for opulently appointed royal trains and wood-paneled, chandeliered saloons pulled by steam engines. The elephant was replaced by the mechanical elephants of the Occident—Rolls-Royces, Hispano-Suizas, and any other motorcar flamboyant enough to catch a jaded ruler's fancy. Where flamboyance was lacking the rulers improvised. The Maharaja of Alwar had a Lancaster built to his personal specifications. The body was shaped like a coronation coach, the chauffeur steered with an ivory steering wheel, and there was an open seat to accommodate two flunkeys at the back of the car. These unique cars, and the fabulous splendor of durbars and state weddings, were captured by an even earlier invention— the camera.

With the advent of the early cameras, photography became a rage in royal India. The Maharaja of Jaipur, Sawai Ram Singh II, was a gifted amateur who specialized in photographic portraits of ladies. His vast harem afforded him a larger choice of subjects than was available to most of his contemporaries. The brilliant photographer to the court of the Nizam of Hyderabad, Deen Dayal, was given a new and resounding title by his appreciative patron— Raja Musavir Jung, "Bold Lion of the Camera."

Fig. 6. *Maharaja Sardar Singh of Jodhpur with Two of His Officers in the Uniforms of the Jodhpur Lancers.* 1903.

Fig. 7. *Maharani Indira of Cooch Behar.*
Painting by A. Jonniaux, Paris, 1932.

Now the Indian rulers were curious to see the lands that produced such inventions. For centuries, however, orthodox Hindus had refused to travel for fear that crossing the *kala pani,* the black waters of the ocean, might pollute their caste. In 1902, when Maharaja Sawai Madho Singh II of Jaipur journeyed to London for the coronation of Edward VII, he avoided such pollution by carrying two huge silver urns filled with the water of the holy river Ganges with which to cleanse himself of the taint of the foreigner. Twenty years later, the Indian rulers were such habitués of Europe that the P. & O. Shipping Line had special suites fitted on its vessels to carry the maharajas through the Suez Canal in the style to which they were accustomed.

The rulers no longer traveled in masculine isolation. Encouraged by the British, the rulers were bringing their ladies out of the harem, and many newly liberated princesses now accompanied their husbands to Europe. Having learned Western refinements from French governesses, these enterprising Indian princesses had acquired, in less than a decade, all the social accomplishments necessary for foreign travel. When they journeyed to the strange world of Europe their clothes were no longer packed in the great dowry chests of the past but in Louis Vuitton cabin trunks. They leaned against the railings of ships in saris made of the lightest French chiffons, a style first popularized by the beautiful Maharani Indira of Cooch Behar. They no longer dabbed attar of roses from fragile Mughal glass containers on themselves but sprayed their bodies with perfumes of the House of Worth from bottles made by Asprey's. They no longer held the jeweled mouthpieces of the hookah between their hennaed fingers. Now an art deco swizzle stick or an ivory cigarette holder dangled from lacquered nails. And their gems were no longer Indian stones set in elaborate enamels but stones from South America set by Cartier.

With exuberant élan the Indian rulers and their princesses indulged themselves in the pleasures offered by Europe. They visited Newmarket to buy thoroughbred horses. They went to Monte Carlo for the gambling. They sailed the Mediterranean. They went to Deauville for the polo and played the game like Europeans, not Mughals.

Dancing was hugely popular with this new breed of cosmopolitan Indian ruler. Although the knowledge of formal ballroom dancing was an essential requirement for viceregal balls, the dashing young Indian princes and princesses much preferred the new dances that were being done in the nightclubs of Paris and London—the tango, the samba, the rhumba. Indeed, a song popular in European capitals at the time pays homage to their dedication to new dance steps.

Fig. 8. *Prince Indrajitendra of Cooch Behar and Princess Kamla of Pitapuram Shortly After Their Wedding.* 1941.

> There was a rich Maharaja of Magador
> Who had ten thousand camels and maybe more
> He had rubies and pearls and the loveliest girls
> But he didn't know how to do the rhumba. . . .

The song has the catchy refrain

> Rhumba lessons are wanted for
> The rich Maharaja of Magador.

By now the traditional Indian courtesan had become something of an anachronism. Princes were bringing their bobbed and bow-lipped European dancing partners home with them. Some maharajas even married their new dancing partners, although the British Empire frowned on

Fig. 9. *Princesses of Kapurthala with H. R. H. Princess Alice of Athlone.* 1930s.

these alliances and refused to consider the issue of such marriages suitable heirs for Indian thrones.

Not all the Indian princes of the time were devoted to the new frivolity. Many took advantage of travel to study at the great European universities. These rulers sent their ablest ministers and councillors abroad for training in administration, law, or finance. Rulers of such kingdoms as Baroda, Bhopal, Mysore, and Travancore ran model states that were the envy of the British administrators of the Indian Empire, and they chafed under the continuing restrictions imposed on them by the empire. In British India, other Indians found British imperialism no less oppressive. Men like Gandhi, who had been partially educated in England, found the vanity of the British colonials and the greed of their industrial machine both irksome and unjust. If asked, they would have described their masters as mere "traders under the purple." With great heroism and personal sacrifice they moved the Indian millions to oust their imperial overlords and in so doing spread the longing for self-government beyond the borders of British India into the heart of the Indian kingdoms. In 1947, when at last the British Union Jack was lowered and the Indian Tricolor flag unfurled, the first Prime Minister of independent India, Jawaharlal Nehru, announced the birth of a nation and the end of princely India with the words "Long years ago we made a tryst with destiny. . . ."

In the final months of their reign many Indian rulers behaved as though nothing had changed. Elegant entertainments were held at Indian courts. In the evenings the gardens glowed with lamps, the fragrance of incense filled the night, and colored fountains played as though time were standing still. Singers and musicians, knowing that

Fig. 10. *Maharaja Sawai Man Singh of Jaipur and Maharani Gayatri Devi.* 1942.

the days of royal patronage were drawing to a close, performed with a last, moving brilliance. A contemporary
poet captured the nostalgia of the moment:

> The time has come for farewells.
> We cannot meet again except in dreams.
> But I shall be reminded of this world
> When I find a faded flower
> Pressed between the pages
> Of a long forgotten book.

In the next year over five hundred Indian kingdoms
merged with the Republic of India. Rulers voluntarily
signed away their ancestral homes and sovereign rights to
spare their people the anguish of civil war. With that last
grand gesture of royal magnanimity they ended the fabled
era of India's courts and kingdoms.

[84.] INTERIOR OF THE TAJ MAHAL. BRITISH PERIOD, CA. 1815.

Commentaries on the Miniatures

1. *Rao Surjan Hada Making Submission to Emperor Akbar in 1568;* outlined by Makand; painted by Shankar; from Abu'l Fazl's *Akbarnama.* Mughal; ca. 1590; 37.5 × 25 cm. Victoria and Albert Museum I.S. 2–1896. 5/117.

In return for submitting to the Mughals, Rao Surjan was exempted from having to prostrate himself before the Emperor and from having to send a daughter to be one of Akbar's wives. He was also given the unique privilege among Rajputs of entering the imperial audience hall fully armed, and he was permitted to sound his kettledrums (*nakkaras*) in the Mughal capital as close as the Red Gate to the fort.

2. *A Mughal and a Rajput Converse in a Garden;* attributable to Basawan. Mughal; ca. 1590; 13 × 7.9 cm. Private collection.

Meeting at dusk in a garden, a Mughal nobleman tries to persuade a proud Rajput to join the imperial cause. In the distance, a peacock slinks through the bushes, echoed in the foreground by a more static bird, in the form of an incense burner. Basawan, a Hindu and Akbar's most brilliant artist, portrayed the distressed Rajput with sympathetic respect. This miniature was slightly enlarged at the edges by the artist.

3. *A Mughal Courtier.* Mughal; ca. 1590; 11.5 × 8.3 cm. Private collection.

Young men eager for service flocked to Akbar's court, where many of them were painted in penetratingly observed characterizations for a royal album. This portrait was probably in the album, which Akbar may have consulted before assigning tasks.

4. *The Feast of Hatim T'ai;* inscribed "at Agra"; from the *Bustan* ("The Garden") of Sa'di; folio 70 recto. Mughal; dated 1609; 9 1/16″ × 4 7/8″. Private collection.

Although the tale illustrated here concerns an Arab chief, one of Jahangir's artists envisioned it in Mughal setting. Dress, tents and awnings, carpet and floorspread, cooking pots and crockery, food and drink—all are accurately rendered from those of the imperial court. The picture describes an Arab renowned for his largesse. When unexpected guests arrived, he served them his finest stallion because his larder was bare.

5. *Wedding Celebrations of Prince Dara Shikoh,* A.D. 1633; from the *Padshahnama;* folio 121 recto. Mughal; ca. 1645; 34.5 × 18.8 cm. Royal Library, Windsor Castle. Copyright reserved. Reproduced by the gracious permission of Her Majesty Queen Elizabeth II.

The marriage in 1633 of Dara Shikoh, Shah Jahan's favorite son and intended heir, was the first joyous celebration at court since the death in 1631 of the Emperor's wife, Mumtaz Mahal, whose white marble tomb, the Taj Mahal, is one of the world's most renowned buildings.

6. *Shah Shuja as an Infant;* by Abu'l Hasan, Nadir al-Zaman ("The Miracle of Time"). Mughal; ca. 1617; 9.3 × 5.3 cm. Private collection.

The favorite grandson of Jahangir, Shah Shuja was painted by the Emperor's most admired artist against a seemingly flat, dark green ground that in fact contains hills and trees. Is the fruit real, or are the mangoes and cherries polychrome toys of the sort still sold in India?

7. *In the Bazaars of Shahjahanabad;* attributable to Bichitr. Mughal; ca. 1645; folio 36.6 × 24.8 cm., miniature 13.6 × 8.2 cm. Private collection.

Merchants, probably from Bukhara in Central Asia, tempt Mughal courtiers with their goods, set up in a characteristic shop near the fort at Delhi. Although unfinished, this unusual view of daily life was mounted in superb floral borders for one of Shah Jahan's albums.

8. *An Abyssinian from Ahmadnagar;* inscribed "the work of Hashim." Mughal; ca. 1633; 15 × 8.1 cm. Private collection.

Abyssinians held high office in India. Fath Khan, shown here, was the son of Malik Ambar, the ruler of Ahmadnagar whose military and statesmanly abilities prevented the Mughals from annexing the Deccani sultanates until after 1633, when the subject of this portrait yielded to Shah Jahan. After being well received at court, Fath Khan was retired to Lahore with a generous allowance.

9. *The Return of Shah Jahan to His Father After the Reduction of Amar Singh;* inscribed "Murad the Painter"; folio 49 recto of the *Padshahnama* ("The History of the Emperor") of 'Abd al-Hamid Lahori, an official history of his reign prepared for Shah Jahan. Mughal; ca. 1645; 34.5 × 18.8 cm. Royal Library, Windsor Castle. Copyright reserved. Reproduced by the gracious permission of Her Majesty Queen Elizabeth II.

Jahangir's eldest son, Prince Khurram, was given the title Shah Jahan ("Sovereign of the World") by his admiring father, who also poured trays of gold coins and jewels over his head in honor of the young man's successful campaigns against the rival rulers of the Deccan. Some years later, angered by the prince's seeming disloyalty, Jahangir referred to him only as Bi-daulat, "Wretch."

10. *A Hindu Girl Dancing.* Deccan, Hyderabad, for a Mughal patron; late seventeenth century; 4¹/16″ × 2⁷/8″. Private collection.

The voluptuous early sculptures of Buddhist *yakshis,* spirits of fertility, inspired the pose and proportions of this greatly appealing miniature, apparently a portrait.

By the late seventeenth century, the Mughals had conquered the Deccani sultanates, and Hyderabad was one of the centers of their power. Mughal and Rajput officers settled there, in Burhanpur, and in Aurangabad, where they maintained lavish establishments.

11. *Celebration of the New Year at the Court of Shah Jahan;* from the *Padshahnama;* folio 70 verso. Mughal; ca. 1645; 34.5 × 18.8 cm.; Royal Library, Windsor Castle. Copyright reserved. Reproduced by the gracious permission of Her Majesty Queen Elizabeth II.

The mood of Shah Jahan's court was rarely excessive. Even here, to the sound of trumpets, *shanais,* drums, and many stringed instruments, imperial dancing-girls move with lively dignity, not abandon.

12. *Wedding Procession.* Mughal, Patna; ca. 1765; 28 × 36.6 cm. Private collection.

Slowly crossing the flat, fertile landscape of Bihar, past familial lands, animals, and *ryots* (cultivators), this stately procession includes the groom on horseback, his father in the howdah of an elephant, and the bride, seemingly a small red and gold bundle, enclosed in her palanquin.

13. *Holi Festival.* Mughal, Oudh; ca. 1765; 18⁵/8″ × 25″. Private collection.

The Hindu festival of Holi celebrates the rites of spring, often in the manner of a saturnalia. Muslims enjoy it, too, as here, humorously dousing and spraying one another with the traditional red liquid made from tesu blossoms, a field of which grows beyond the marble terrace of a garden set in a lake. The patron, surrounded by flowers, sweetmeats, and extra "ammunition," enjoys the antics of his courtiers, dancing-girls, and clowns.

14. *Entertainment in a Harem Garden;* inscribed "the work of Faiz-ullah." Mughal, Oudh, Faizabad; ca. 1765; 50.3 × 69.2 cm. Private collection.

In his painted Mughal paradise on earth, Faiz-ullah envisioned the harem of a great late Mughal palace complex peopled with the ruler's wives and their attendants. In the distance, beyond architectural vistas sprinkled with vanishing points and a river lively with horse- and dragon-prowed boats, the nawab enjoys a hunt.

15. *Senior Wives Playing Chaupar in the Court Zenana with Eunuchs;* possibly by Navasi Lal after a lost original by Tilly Kettle. Mughal, Lucknow; ca. 1790; 18 × 10.5 cm. James Ivory Collection.

Lucknow and Hyderabad eventually surpassed Delhi in grandeur—and in inspired folly—during the long, slow decline of the Mughal Empire, which began in 1739, when Nadir Shah invaded from Persia, and ended with the exile to Rangoon in Burma of Emperor Bahadur Shah II (ruled 1837–1858) following the India Mutiny. During the late eighteenth century, English artists, such as Tilly Kettle, were lavishly rewarded for painting portraits at Lucknow, and variations on these orientalist canvasses flowered in local ateliers.

16. *Courtesan After Bathing.* Mughal, Delhi or Alwar; ca. 1815; 9 9/16″ × 6″. James Ivory Collection.

Regency exotica appealed to the later Mughals much as chinoiserie delighted Europeans and Americans. Corinthian columns, an English table, and an ornamental "parade" of little European pictures spice this indelicate peep at a courtesan, a very shocking subject when it was painted.

17. *The Courtesan Who Loved Cats.* Mughal, Lucknow; ca. 1835; 11 7/16″ × 7 12/16″. James Ivory Collection.

Courtesans in India were often highly educated ladies of immense charm, trained in the manner of Japan's geishas to converse wittily, to sing, and to dress with extreme elegance.

18. *A Courtesan Ready for Visitors.* Mughal, Lucknow; ca. 1835; 9 5/16″ × 6 8/16″. James Ivory Collection.

Sets of painted portraits, and later of photographs, showing admired courtesans were eagerly acquired by amateurs of the arts.

19. *Some of the King's Women.* Mughal, Lucknow; ca. 1815; 33 × 32 cm. Private collection.

Savagely, perhaps improvingly, ripped through the face of its patron, King Ghazzi-ud-din (who is shown reviewing a few of the ladies of his harem from a barge), this florid miniature dramatically expresses the ambiance of Lucknow at the time when the British spited the Mughal Emperor by honoring their Lucknow puppet with a title deemed higher than his. The Italian marble sculpture on the riverbank typifies Lucknow's hybrid taste.

20. *A Nawab from Lucknow* (Nawab Muzaffar-ud-daulah Nasir al-Mulk Mirza Sa'if-ud-din Haidar Khan Bahadur Saif Jang). Mughal, Delhi; dated 1852; 36.5 × 25 cm. Private collection.

A patron of poetry and the arts, this friend of Ghalib, the last great Mughal man of letters, fled from Delhi to avoid the terrors of the India Mutiny of 1857. His palace was ransacked and burned; and in the aftermath of the troubles, he was arrested by British officers at Alwar, taken to Gurgaon, and without investigation or inquiry shot dead.

21. *An Elegant Painter from Jaipur;* by Suraj Baksh. Mughal work at Jaipur, Rajasthan; dated 1869; 8 1/16″ × 5 5/16″. Ismail Merchant Collection.

This old-fashioned Muslim artist, presumably trained in the Delhi workshops, was probably employed in the ateliers of Maharaja Ram Singh II of Jaipur.

22. *Palanquin Carried by Red-coated Bearers.* British Period, Patna; mid-1800s; 5 12/16″ × 7 12/16″. James Ivory Collection.

The bazaars of Patna developed a local school of painting in which Mughal and English modes blended to satisfy traditional Indian as well as foreign clients. Subjects such as this one especially pleased English customers, who acquired them as souvenirs.

23. *Kaiserbagh Palace;* Mughal, Lucknow; mid-1800s; 21 3/8″ × 37 1/2″. Private collection.

"The king is a crazy imbecile," wrote W. H. Sleeman, the distinguished civil servant and author of *A Journey Through the Kingdom of Oudh in 1849–50* of Nawab Wajid 'Ali Shah (ruled 1847–1856), who is being carried through his palace grounds in this large, fossil-like painting. A lover of poetry, music, and dancing-girls, Wajid

'Ali blunderingly attempted to strengthen Oudh's army —for which he was exiled to Calcutta by the British.

24. Rana Amar Singh II (ruled 1698–1710) at Prayer. Rajput, Mewar; ca. 1698; 51.3 × 39 cm. Private collection.

Rana Amar Singh II, who could trace his ancestry back to the sun, was known in the chronicles as a "high-minded prince, who well upheld his station and the prosperity of his country." Here, his right hand turns his prayer beads inside a cloth bag *(gomukhi)* used in Vaishnavite worship. Although his reign was brief, he directed his artists in excitingly new directions.

25. Rao Jagat Singh I of Kotah (ruled 1658–1670) in His Garden. Rajput, Kotah; ca. 1670; 10½″ × 7³/8″. Private collection.

Rao Jagat served the Mughal Emperor Aurangzeb during the Deccani campaigns; while there he hired a remarkable artist from Golconda, whose extraordinary draughtsmanship change the course of Kotah art. One of his earliest paintings for his new patron, this portrait of Rao Jagat represents Rajput nobility at its lively best.

26. Princess Admiring a Bird. Punjab Hills, Basohli; ca. 1675; 14.6 × 18.4 cm. Private collection.

In the remote Punjab Hills, a smolderingly powerful traditional style survived at the Rajput court of Basohli until the late seventeenth century, uninfluenced by Mughal example. Like pre-Mughal Rajput pictures from Rajasthan, this one retains strong links to an ancient pan-Indian mode in which expressive intensity outweighed naturalism. The artist of this picture, like a virtuoso musician, proudly drew in a graceful single hair, snaking its way down the princess's cheek, with a single, masterful slither of the brush.

27. Raja Jai Singh of Sawar with Female Musicians. Rajput, Ajmer; ca. 1690; 10″ × 19″. Private collection.

Although the strains of Raja Jai's melodic ladies will never again be heard, their peculiarly ornamental turbans, doelike faces, and graceful attitudes continue to please, thanks to the raja's artist, whose line and color are so "musical" that we almost hear the plucked strings and voices.

28. Prince and Ladies Shooting Heron from a Terrace; attributable to Ustad Murad. Rajput, Bikaner; ca. 1710; 9⁷/8″ × 6⁷/8″. Private collection.

As at Kotah and Kishangarh, the ateliers of Bikaner profited from the service of its rulers in the Deccan, where Rao Anup Singh (ruled 1669–1698) captured and later governed the great fort of Adoni. The nostalgic lassitude of the defeated Deccani sultanates permeates the works of Ustad ("Master") Murad, as in this depiction of the successful marksmanship of Rao Sujan Singh (ruled 1700–1735), a mighty hunter, even in the *zenana* (harem) garden.

29. Todi Ragini; from a *Ragamala* ("Garland of Melody"). Rajput, Kotah; ca. 1700; 7³/8″ × 4½″. Private collection.

Ragamala sets, usually of thirty-six pictures, were painted at most Rajput courts. Each traditional subject represents a musical mode or theme and is suited to a specific season, time of day or night, and mood. This miniature, with its charming heroine and sprightly animals, can be attributed to the Kotah Master (see Plates 25 and 32).

30. Jyeshtha: The Hot Month; attributable to Ustad Murad as an old man. Rajput, Bikaner; ca. 1725; 10⅛″ × 6⁵/8″. Private collection.

From a *Baramasa* series, describing the ways of lovers during the twelve months of the year, this one depicts the time of heat so terrible that the elephant tolerates its natural enemy the snake. Ustad Murad's parched palette and the attenuated proportions of the figures effectively raise the temperature of this miniature.

31. Rama Hunting by Moonlight; signed by Bhimsen. Rajput, Kotah; dated 1781; 8⁷/8″ × 10¹⁵/16″. Private collection.

The blue god is depicted in the guise of a Kotah prince, perhaps Maharao Umed Singh (ruled 1771–1819), the patron of a new group of Hindu artists, such as Bhimsen, who worked in a broader, less linear style than those trained in the workshop rooted in Deccani style. Hunting scenes continued to be the specialty of the Kotah school.

32. *Rao Ram Singh I of Kotah (ruled 1686–1708) Chases a Rhinoceros.* Rajput, Kotah; ca. 1695; 12¼″ × 18⁷/₁₆″. Private collection.

Also by the artist known as "the Kotah Master," this miniature is unsurpassed in conveying the surge and power of a running elephant, whose whiplashing bell-ropes were observed with the utmost empathy. The rhinoceros was hunted in Rajasthan until soon after 1700.

33. *Lion Hunt.* Rajput, Kishangarh; ca. 1735; 6⁵/₈″ × 10¹⁵/₁₆″. James Ivory Collection.

The ruling house of Kishangarh, a cadet branch of the Rathors of Marwar, developed a remarkable atelier of artists, apparently recruited from imperial Delhi and the Deccan. Subtle draughtsmen and colorists, the Kishangarh artists followed their patrons' tastes for expressive, often unsettling, occasionally dreamlike interpretations of Rajput life.

34. *By the Light of the Moon, Lamps, and Fireworks;* attributable to Nihal Chand. Rajput, Kishangarh; ca. 1740; 21.8 × 15.6 cm. Private collection.

Outrageous comedy, satire, and perceptive reportage intertwine in this record of a nocturnal orgy, presided over by a blowsy and intoxicated graybeard. Painted with astonishing verve and refinement by a masterful artist reminiscent of Goya, such documentation of excesses would not have been tolerated at the Mughal court—not even by Emperor Mohammed Shah (ruled 1719–1748), known as "the Pleasure-lover" *(Rangila),* who was a friend of the Kishangarh prince.

35. *Longing.* Rajput, Bundi; mid-1700s; 9⁹/₁₆″ × 6³/₈″. Fogg Art Museum, Harvard University, gift of John Kenneth Galbraith.

Rajput miniatures underscore the painful languor of the *zenana,* where women sighed for lovers preoccupied by hunting and soldiering. The lunar palette of whites accented with brilliant colors—perhaps inspired by Shah Jahan's marble palaces—isolates the waiting Rajputni and intensifies her brooding state.

36. *Lovers Strolling by a Pool.* Punjab Hills, Kangra; ca. 1780; 6³/₈″ × 4″. Private collection.

Kangra artists usually saw the world as paradise. This aristocratically perfect couple stroll in a garden enclosed by *shamianas* (cloth screens), attended by beautiful, sensitively mannered servants. After taking the air round a pond, they will ascend the ramp and enter an awninged pavilion to sip wine or sherbet, eat sweetmeats, and talk of love.

37. *Lady Playing a Tanpura.* Punjab Hills, Kangra style at Basohli; ca. 1780; 10³/₄″ × 7¹/₁₆″. Courtesy of the Fogg Art Museum, Harvard University, gift of John Kenneth Galbraith.

At Kangra and related schools in the eighteenth century, a gently poetic, linear style blended Rajput expressiveness with naturalistic Mughal nuances. At its best, as in the examples of Kangra style we illustrate, this potentially cloying idiom achieved Botticellian grace; at worst, it rivals the bathos of valentines.

38. *Baby Worship: A Family at Play.* Punjab Hills, Kangra style at Datarpur; early 1800s; 7¹/₂″ × 5″. James Ivory Collection.

Framed by an elegant archway, parents disport with their Krishna-like infant son. Rain clouds gather, bringing cooling winds across the lake and auguring goodly harvests.

39. *The Month of Rain.* Punjab Hills, Kangra; ca. 1810; 9¹/₄″ × 7″. Private collection.

Left over from the hot month, ripe mangoes still hang from the trees as the waterbirds swoop through the air and the monsoon rains begin to fall, swelling the river. In the upper room of the palace, startled by a lightning bolt (symbolic of ecstacy), the beloved reaches out for her bold lover.

40. *A Day at Gagraun Fort.* Rajput, Kotah; ca. 1735; 55 × 73.1 cm. Private collection.

The "heart" of a larger drawing, this schematic view of the massive fort that guarded the southern borders of Kotah state shows Maharao Durjan Sal of Kotah (ruled 1723–56) watching elephants combat while receiving salutations from his officers. At the left, an elephant disappears up the ramp of a side gate. The artist, a follower of the Kotah Master, conveys the effect of sunlight on rugged masonry.

41. *Durbar Hall.* Unidentified Maratha school; ca. 1820; 31.5 × 24.5 cm. Private collection.

With the weakening of Mughal power, the Marathas spread from their homelands in the Deccan and established principalities in many parts of northern India. Wearing a characteristic Maratha turban and smoking his *huqqa* (hookah), this royal personage gives audience in the perspective of a splendid hall of whitewashed stone enriched with blue and white striped *daris* (dhurries), carpets, and imported glass oil lamps.

42. *Maharaja Man Singh of Jodhpur (ruled 1804–1843) Sniffs a Pink.* Rajput, Marwar; early 1800s; 9⁹/16″ × 7¹¹/16″. James Ivory Collection.

Maharajas fortunate enough to live far away from British centers of power enjoyed a short-lived Rajput renaissance during the years of Mughal decline. Man Singh's artist, forswearing Mughal naturalism, has abstracted the royal features into powerfully decorative natural forms, as in the attenuated, leaf-shaped eye. Balancing the flower, the maharaja holds a dagger *(katar)* in his left hand. Both symbolize traits of his cheerful, at times ruthless, personality.

43. *A Sikh Prince and Tutor in a Pavilion During the Monsoon.* Punjab, probably Lahore; ca. 1835; 10¹⁵/16″ × 9⁸/16″. Private collection.

The Sikhs are a sect of reformist Hindus founded by Guru Nanak (1469–1539), who had been strongly influenced by Kabir, a holy man whose beliefs contained those of Hinduism and Islam. Under "the Lion of the Punjab," Maharaja Ranjit Singh (1780–1839), the Sikhs controlled most of the Punjab and held out staunchly and effectively against the British.

Hira Singh, the favorite and virtually adopted son of Ranjit Singh, is shown here as a young man.

44. *Prithvi Singh of Kishangarh (ruled 1840–1880) Riding with His Son, Sardul Singh.* Rajput, Kishangarh; dated 1841; 15⁷/16″ × 11¹¹/16″. Private collection.

Colonel G. B. Malleson wrote in 1875, thirty-five years after Prithvi Singh's accession to the *gaddi* (throne) of Kishangarh, "since that time nothing has occurred worthy of special notice." He observes elsewhere, however, that the raja's father, Kalian Singh, "employed himself [at Delhi] in buying honorary privileges from the king, such as the right to wear stockings in the royal presence." The colonel's opinions reflect British dismay in the aftermath of the Mutiny of 1857.

45. *A Boy Maharaja of Indore in Durbar.* Central India, Indore; ca. 1850; 20⁴/16″ × 16²/16″. James Ivory Collection.

Tukaji Rao Holkar, ten years old when the state of Indore was conferred upon him by the British Governor-General, was painted in an aerie-like durbar hall adorned with Victorian chandeliers, a ceiling painted with gold foliage, and mirrors that reflect the cloudy sky and hurricane lamps. He attained his majority in 1852 and was awarded the Star of India in 1862. He was entitled by the British to a salute of nineteen guns.

46. *Boy King with Brahmin Priest.* Kotah; 1880. James Ivory Collection.

Maharo Umed Singh of Kotah, who came to the throne as a boy in 1889, is revered in a pavilion. Although his movable garden of potted flowers and the architecture are traditional, the cheval glass and his overstuffed throne are offerings from overseas.

55. *A Muslim Courtesan;* signed "The work of Gopilal the Painter." Rajput, Marwar, Jodhpur; ca. 1875; 20.1 × 14.1 cm. Private collection.

Seated bolt upright on a formal gilt chair, an old-fashioned Muslim lady, wearing a framed miniature of her lover (probably the maharaja), poses for her portrait. But did she face a camera or a painter? Despite the artists' struggles, photography increased in popularity in Rajasthan, and Gopilal's style, as represented here, so bowed to the vogue for the camera that his sitter appears to have reacted to the lensman's request to "hold that pose." Probably the artist based his likeness on a photograph.

68. *Maharajas of Rajasthan.* Ca. 1865; 15⁴/16″ × 108/16″. Ismail Merchant Collection.

Painted at a time when artists were threatened and influenced by photography, this portrait demonstrated that masters of the brush could hold their own against magicians of the lens. Not only was the sitter spared the hazards of exposing body and soul to a little-known, possibly lethal device, but he could be placed by his courteous painter in whatever surroundings he desired.

72. *A Sikh Ruler, Perhaps the Maharaja of Patiala.* Punjab, Sikh school; ca. 1885; 10 1/2″ × 8″. Paul F. Walter Collection.

Beneath European angels—borrowed from Mughal portraiture, which in turn had adapted them from European sources—a stout, richly jeweled, Sikh-turbaned maharaja occupies an oval set against a Victorian pastiche of floral arabesques and reverential tigers.

74. *Nawab Asaf-ud-daulah of Oudh (ruled 1775–1797);* watercolor from the album of Mr. George Adams of the Bengal Civil Service. Bengal, Calcutta; ca. 1826; 36.5 × 23.1 cm. Private collection.

Decades after his death, the legendary Mughal Nawab of Oudh was painted for a large album made for an English civil servant by an artist whose fantasies at times resemble those of Saul Steinberg.

75. *Nadir Shah of the Afsharid Dynasty of Persia (ruled 1736–1747);* watercolor from the album of Mr. George Adams. Bengal, Calcutta; ca. 1826; 36.5 × 23.1 cm. Private collection.

The illustrious Peacock Throne and caravan-loads of other Mughal spoils were hauled away to Persia by Nadir Shah, the scourge of Delhi—and of Emperor Mohammed Shah (ruled 1719–1748), who was avenged eighty-seven years later by Mr. Adams's Calcutta artist when he painted this spritely likeness.

81. *The Last Mughal Emperor, Bahadur Shah II, with Two Sons; The Heir Apparent, Fakhrud-din Mirza at His Right, and Mirza Farkhanda.* Mughal, North India, Delhi; dated in the month of Rabi I, A.H. 1254 (May–June 1838); 32 × 38 cm. Private collection.

On this final great imperial Mughal portrait are inscribed some of his honorifics: "The Shadow of God," "Exalted King of Kings," "Refuge of Islam," and "Increasor of the Splendour of the Community of the Paraclete." The lions supporting the throne are scrawny and feeble and the Emperor's halo has turned from the usual gold to hauntingly anemic pale blues.

83. *Interior of the Tomb of Etahmadolah (Itimad-ud-daulah);* watercolor. British Period; ca. 1815; 48 × 63 cm. Paul F. Walter Collection.

This richly adorned chamber contains the gravestones of Itimad-ud-daulah and his wife, parents of Nur Jahan, wife of Jahangir, and aunt of Mumtaz Mahal, who was married to Shah Jahan. One of India's most beautiful tombs, it was built with jewel-like richness under Nur Jahan's patronage between 1622 and 1628.

84. *Interior of the Taj Mahal;* watercolor. British Period; ca. 1815; border 47 × 63 cm.; image size (arched top) 44 × 31 cm. Paul F. Walter Collection.

Through the archway of the screens *(jalis)* one sees the inlaid marble cenotaph of Empress Mumtaz Mahal, the wife of Shah Jahan, who died in 1631 while bearing her fourteenth child. In accord with Muslim custom, her remains are buried in the earth, near those of Shah Jahan, beneath an inlaid marble gravestone in a vault directly under the cenotaph. Pictures of this sort were made at Agra by artists trained in the Mughal tradition for sale to British visitors.

Costume Glossary

Men (upper body)

Achkan
Angarkha
Balabar
Chadar *
Chapkan
Choga
Doshala or Dhoshala *
Jama
Kaftan
Kurta
Nima
Patka
Shal
Shaluka
Sherwani

Men (lower body)

Cudidara Pajama *
Dhoti
Gharara *
Lungi
Pajama *
Salwar *

Caps

Chau Goshia
Dopatri or Dopalli
Kullah or Kula
Mandil
Nukka Dar
Topi

Turbans

Balaband
Dastar
Pag or Pagri
Sapha or Saph
Shimla or Shamla

Shoes and Slippers

Charndharan
Ghatela
Kafsh
Kurd Nau
Salim Shahi

Women (upper body)

Angya-Kurti
Chadar *
Choli
Doshala *
Duppata
Jaguli
Kurti
Orhni
Peshwaz or Paswaz

Women (lower body)

Cudidara Pajama *
Ghaghra
Gharara *
Pajama *
Phentia
Salwar *
Sari
Zaraband

*Worn by both
men and women

GARMENTS

ACHKAN: a long coat, which is tightly buttoned from neck to waist, open to the knees, and slit at the sides (Pl. 51, 76).

ANGARKHA: a long, fitted coat or overcoat (meaning protector of the body), often richly decorated, worn with a belt or sash. A lune-shaped piece of material, known as a kantha, lies over the chest (Pl. 59, 68).

BALABAR: a coat, less full-skirted than the JAMA, with a broad band (gusset) at the right edge that hooks on the left to keep it closed. The collar is cut round and low to show an inner jacket (Pl. 20). (In Lucknow this inner vestment is known as a SHALUKA.)

CHADAR: a mantle or heavy shawl.

CHAPKAN: a winter coat usually made of wool or thick cloth, in vogue in the late nineteenth century. It is similar to the ANGARKHA but shorter with tighter sleeves (when the sleeves are too long or tight, they are slit or gathered in folds). The insert piece, the kantha, is fastened by buttons over the chest. Often a row of buttons forms a decorative bow-shaped edge along one side (Pl. 67).

CHOGA: a long, formal coat of the nineteenth century, made of rich material and sometimes heavily embroidered. It opens in the front, is V-necked, and is usually fastened by two buttons (Pl. 80).

CHOLI: a close-fitting woman's bodice, usually with short sleeves; fastened in the back or front (Pl. 10).

CUDIDARA PAJAMA: long pants whose name, *cudi,* meaning "brace-

let," is derived from tapering legs that form braceletlike folds near the ankles. These are the ancestors of what we know of as jodhpurs (Pl. 25, 69).

DHOSHALA or DOSHALA: a cotton or wool shawl from Akbar's time that had only two lengthwise folds, rather than the customary four. At a later period the name also came to mean the heavy brocaded shawls popular in Lucknow (Pl. 3, 17).

DHOTI: a cloth wrapped around the lower body with one end passing between the legs and tucked in at the back of the waist. The traditional dress of the Indian, worn at home and at worship (Pl. 24).

DUPPATA: a mantle similar to the ORHNI. It means "two pieces," sewn together side by side. At times one end is tucked into the front of the skirt, forming a decorative panel, similar to the PHENTIA.

GHAGHRA or GHAGRA: a skirt or petticoat. Abu'l Fazl, in Akbar's reign, describes Hindu women as wearing a lower garment, or waist-cloth, which is joined at both ends by a band and sewn at the top where the cord for fastening passes (Pl. 25, 28).

GHARARA: loose baggy trousers worn by men and women. Those worn by women are at times so wide that they cover the feet and have to be carried like a train (Pl. 17, 18).

JAGULI: a high-waisted dress derived from the Mughals that has long, tight-fitting sleeves and a long, flowing skirt. Although fastened at the neck and waist, an opening allows a glimpse of the breasts. This dress, associated with the Punjab Hills, is seen in Kangra painting (Pl. 37).

JAMA: a coat or long tunic with a

full skirt, whose length varied according to fashion. It was gathered at the waist by a belt or sash (PATKA). For Hindus, the outer flap covering the chest fastens with tapes at the left armpit; for Muslims, it fastens at the right (there are exceptions). The flap over the chest is called a pardah, meaning "curtain" (Pl. 2).

KAFTAN: a short-sleeved, gaudily colored vest that is worn over a JAMA (Pl. 11).

KURTA: an upper-body garment; a tunic or shirt with long sleeves.

KURTI: a blouse or overblouse for women. An ANGYA-KURTI is a combination of blouse and vest worn underneath a PESHWAZ.

LUNGI: a cloth wrapped one or more times around the hips and tucked into the waist. It is the traditional Muslim dress at home, comparable to the Hindu DHOTI.

NIMA: a half-sleeved garment worn under the JAMA.

ORHNI: a mantle, head covering, or scarf of various lengths, often diaphanous; the end is sometimes tucked into the skirt in front (Pl. 28).

PAJAMA: (from the Hindi *paejama,* which means "leg clothing") loose trousers, tied around the waist and worn by both men and women. Three varieties are CUDIDARA, GHARARA, and SALWAR (Pl. 26).

PATKA: a sash or belt whose extremely elaborate ends, woven or embroidered, add a strong decorative accent to the costume (Pl. 8).

PESHWAZ or PASWAZ: a diaphanous full-skirted gown, often with short sleeves, introduced by the Mughals. It is open in front, sometimes with ties, revealing the PA-

JAMA underneath. Originally presented as a ceremonial gift from the Imperial Court to daughters of royal houses, it was so admired that it was adopted by royalty and dancing-girls alike (Pl. 26).

PHENTIA: a long panel of contrasting material that hangs down the front of the skirt, giving the effect of a sash; it is thought to be a descendant of the medieval cloth girdle. The ORHNI or DUPPATA, when tucked into the front of a skirt, has a similar effect (Pl. 29).

SALWAR PAJAMA: baggy or loose trousers, slightly gathered at the ankle; when worn by Punjab women, they are called suthan (Pl. 26).

SARI: the traditional unstitched garment worn by women. In early times it was the word for the cloth wrapped around the lower body (similar to a man's DHOTI or LUNGI) and was accompanied by a similar cloth wrapping the upper body (like the DUPPATA and the ORHNI). In time, its size so increased that this one piece assumed both functions, covering both upper and lower body: the SARI we know today (Pl. 64).

SHAL: a length of cotton or wool, with or without border, folded lengthwise and wrapped around the shoulders with one end hanging over the forearm. SHAL, from Akbar's time, has given us our contemporary "shawl" (Pl. 3).

SHALUKA: a colored undervest, popular in Lucknow.

SHERWANI: a long coat similar to an ACHKAN but with a collar; it developed into the formal male attire of modern India (Pl. 51).

ZARABAND: a cord at the waist of the GHARARA; richly tassled ends extend below the knees (Pl. 35).

CAPS AND TURBANS

BALABAND: a decorative band, or silken fillet, wound transversely around the turban (Pl. 3).

CHAU GOSHIA: a dome-shaped, four-cornered cap, traditional in Delhi and Lucknow during the nineteenth century.

DASTAR: a name given to the turban in Akbar's time, made of various lengths of silk or cotton, which were twisted and then wrapped around a cap or KULLAH. It also refers to a turban of fine muslin worn by Delhi nobles of a later period (Pl. 80).

DOPALRI or DOPALLI: a cap consisting of two lune-shaped pieces of cloth with a seam down the middle, often embroidered (Pl. 80).

KULLAH or KULA: a pointed skull cap, around which the cloth of the turban is wound.

MANDIL: a stiff drum-shaped cap decorated with gold or silver embroidery (Pl. 21).

NUKKA DAR: a small, narrow cap, pointed back and front, which evolved from the DOPALRI; it is heavily decorated with gold and silver embroidery.

PAG or PAGRI: an asymmetrical turban with a contrasting decorative band (BALABAND); presumably of Rajput origin, it was adopted by the Mughals at the time of Akbar (Pl. 3).

SAPHA or SAPH: a turban or man's headdress comprising various lengths of cloth wound around the head, sometimes over a cap or KULLAH. The manner of tying it denotes a social position and culture.

SHIMLA or SHAMLA: a kind of turban consisting of a circlet of fine wide cloth fitted to the head and open at the crown. Long twisted folds of silk or brocade are wound around and sewn on the circlet at the top and bottom. A broad band of similar material is attached above to hold the folds in place. Since this does not cover the whole head, a cap or DOPALRI is worn underneath. This form of turban is thought to have been inspired by the courtly headdresses of central India and became popular in Lucknow in 1800; its influence then spread to Murshidabad and Calcutta (Pl. 20).

TOPI: a cap or hat.

FOOTWEAR

CHARHWAN or CHARNDHARAN: a shoe consisting of a leather piece covering the outer portion of the foot (toes, instep, and sole); a piece of leather is added to cover the entire heel up to the ankle. In time it became known as "the Delhi shoe," as it is thought to have originated there.

GHATELA: a shoe with a large toe piece curling back over the foot, at times so large as to resemble an elephant's trunk (Pl. 20).

KAFSH: a Persian-style high-heeled sandal.

KURD NAU: this shoe, a style that originated in Lucknow, has a rounded-off toe cap; it is made of brightly colored velvets and brocades for the dry season; for the wet season, it is made of shagreen (Pl. 76).

SALIM SHAHI: a slipper with a pointed toe sometimes tilted inward. It originated during the time of Jahangir (Prince Salim), hence its name; in later periods it was decorated with gold and silver threads (Pl. 30).

Bibliography

HISTORICAL WORKS: PRIMARY SOURCES

Abu'l Fazl Allami. *A'in-i-Akbari.* Translated by H. Blochmann and H. Jarett. Calcutta, 1875–1948.

———. *Akbarnama.* Translated by H. Blochmann. Calcutta, 1907.

Babur. *The Baburnama in English.* Translated by A. S. Beveridge. London, 1969.

Bernier, François. *Travels in the Mughal Empire (1656–1668).* Edited by A. Constable. London, 1891.

Devi, Gayatri, and Santha Rama Rau. *A Princess Remembers: The Memoirs of the Maharani of Jaipur.* New York, 1985.

Eden, Emily. *Up the Country: Letters Written to Her Sister from the Upper Provinces of India.* Edited by E. J. Thompson. Oxford, 1930.

Heber, Reginald. *Narrative of a Journey through the Upper Provinces of India, from Calcutta to Bombay, 1824–1825.* 2nd ed. London, 1828.

Hickey, William. *Memoirs.* Edited and debowdlerized by Peter Quennell under the title *The Prodigal Rake.* New York, 1962.

Jahangir. *The Tuzuk-i-Jahangiri; or Memoirs of Jahangir.* Translated by A. Rogers and edited by H. Beveridge. London, 1909–14.

Knighton, William. *The Private Life of an Eastern King.* London, 1856.

MacKenzie, Mrs. Colin. *Life in the Mission, the Camp and the Zenana or Six Years in India.* London, 1854.

Meer, Mrs. Hassan 'Ali. *Observations on the Mussulmans of India.* 1832, reprinted Karachi, 1974.

Parks, Fanny. *The Wanderings of a Pilgrim in Search of the Picturesque during Four-and-Twenty Years in the East.* 1850, reprinted Lahore, 1975.

Roe, Thomas. *Embassy of Sir Thomas Roe to India, 1615–1619.* Edited by William Foster. London and New York, 1926.

Sleeman, William H. *Rambles and Recollections of an Indian Official.* 2 vols. London, 1844.

Tavernier, Jean Baptiste. *Travels in India.* Edited by W. Crooke. Oxford, 1925.

Tod, James. *The Annals and Antiquities of Rajasthan.* Edited by W. Crooke. London, 1920.

SECONDARY SOURCES

Alexander, Michael, and Svshila Anand. *Queen Victoria's Maharajah Duleep Singh 1838–93.* London, 1980.

Bence-Jones, Mark. *Palaces of the Raj: Magnificence and Misery of the Lord Sahibs.* London, 1973.

Chaudhuri, Nirad C. *The Continent of Circe.* Bombay, 1974.

Duff, James Grant. *A History of the Mahrattas.* Edited by J. P. Guha. Delhi, 1971.

Edwardes, Michael. *Bound to Exile: The Victorians in India.* London, 1969.

———. *The Orchid House: Splendours and Miseries of the Kingdom of Oudh 1827–1857.* London, 1960.

Galbraith, Katherine Atwater, and Rama Mehta. *India.* Boston, 1980.

Gascoigne, Bamber. *The Great Moghuls.* London, 1971.

Godden, Rumer. *Gulbadan: Portrait of a Rose Princess at the Mughal Court.* New York, 1981.

Golish, Vitold de. *Splendeurs et Crépuscules des Maharajas.* Paris, 1963.

Hambly, Gavin. *Cities of Mughal India: Delhi, Agra, and Fatehpur Sikri.* Photographs by Wim Swaan. New York, 1968.

Holkar, Shivaji Rao, and Shalini Devi Holkar. *Cooking of the Maharajahs.* New York, 1975.

Ivory, James. *Autobiography of a Princess.* New York, 1975.

Jeffrey, Robin, ed. *People, Princes and Paramount Power; Society and Politics in the Indian Princely States.* Oxford, 1978.

Lord, John. *The Maharajahs.* London, 1971.

Moynihan, Elizabeth B. *Paradise as a Garden in Persia and Mughal India.* New York, 1979.

Sarkar, J. *History of Aurangzeb.* Calcutta, 1925.

Singh, Khushwant. *A History of the Sikhs,* Vol. I: *1469–1839.* Oxford, 1963.

Spear, Percival. *The Nabobs: A Study of the Social Life of the English in Eighteenth-Century India.* Rev. ed. Oxford, 1963.

————. *Twilight of the Mughuls: Studies in Late Mughul Delhi.* Cambridge, 1951.

Woodruff, Philip. *The Men Who Ruled India,* Vol. I: *The Founders.* Vol. II: *The Guardians.* New York, 1954.

WORKS RELATING TO INDIAN PAINTING

Archer, Mildred. *Company Drawings in the India Office Library.* London, 1972.

————, and William G. Archer. *Indian Painting for the British 1770–1880.* Oxford, 1955.

Archer, William G. *Indian Paintings from the Punjab Hills.* 2 vols. London, New York, and Delhi, 1973.

————. *Visions of Courtly India.* London, New York, Delhi, and Karachi, 1976.

————, and Edwin C. Binney 3rd. *Rajput Miniatures from the Collection of Edwin C. Binney 3rd.* Portland, Ore., 1968.

Arnold, T. W. *The Library of A. Chester Beatty: A Catalogue of the Indian Miniatures.* Revised and edited by J. V. S. Wilkinson. Oxford, 1936.

Barr, Pat, and Ray Desmond. *Simla; Hill Station in British India.* London, 1978.

Barrett, D., and B. Gray, *Painting of India.* Lausanne, 1963.

Beach, Milo C. *The Adventures of Rama.* Washington, D.C., 1983.

————. *The Grand Mogul; Imperial Painting in India 1600–1660.* Williamstown, Mass., 1978.

————. *The Imperial Image; Painting for the Mughal Court.* Washington, D.C., 1981.

————. *Rajput Painting at Bundi and Kota.* Ascona, 1974.

Brown, P. *Indian Painting under the Mughals.* Oxford, 1924.

Desmond, Ray. *Victorian India in Focus.* London, 1982.

Ettinghausen, Richard. *Paintings of the Sultans and Emperors of India in American Collections.* New Delhi, 1961.

Khandalavala, K., and M. Chandra. *New Documents of Indian Painting—A Reappraisal.* Bombay, 1969.

Lall, John. *Taj Mahal and the Glory of Mughal Agra.* New Delhi, 1982.

Pal, Pratapaditya. *The Classical Tradition in Rajput Painting: From the Paul F. Walter Collection.* New York, 1978.

Randhawa, Mohinder Singh, and John Kenneth Galbraith. *Indian Painting; The Scene, Themes and Legends.* Boston, 1968.

Schimmel, Anne Marie, and Stuart Cary Welch. *Anvari's Divan; A Pocket Book for Akbar.* New York, 1983.

Skelton, Robert. *The Indian Heritage; Court Life and Arts under Mughal Rule.* London, 1982.

Stchoukine, I. "Un Bustan de Sadi Illustré par des Artistes Moghols," *Revue des Arts Asiatiques* 9 (1937): 2.

————. *La Peinture Indienne.* Paris, 1929.

Topsfield, Andrew. *Paintings from Rajasthan in the National Gallery of Victoria.* Melbourne, 1980.

Welch, Stuart Cary. *The Art of Mughal India.* New York, 1963.

————. *Imperial Mughal Painting.* New York, 1978.

————. *Indian Drawings and Painted Sketches.* New York, 1976.

————. *A King's Book of Kings.* New York, 1972.

————. *Room for Wonder.* New York, 1978.

————, and Milo C. Beach. *Gods, Thrones, and Peacocks.* New York, 1965.

————, and M. Zebrowski. *A Flower from Every Meadow.* New York, 1964.

BIBLIOGRAPHY

COLOR PLATE AND PHOTOGRAPHIC BOOKS

Baroda, Maharaja of. *The Palaces of India.* London, 1980.

Beny, Roloff, and Sylvia A. Matheson. *Rajasthan.* London, 1984.

———, and Aubrey Menen. *India.* New York, 1969.

Cameron, Roderick. *Shadows from India; An Architectural Album.* London, 1958.

Hendley, Thomas H. *The Rulers of India and the Chiefs of Rajputana.* London, 1897.

Jahangir, Sorabji. *Princes and Chiefs of India.* London, 1903.

Singh, Raghubir. *Kashmir.* New York, 1983.

———. *Rajasthan.* New York, 1981.

———, and Joseph Lelyveld. *Calcutta.* Hong Kong, 1975.

Worswick, Clark. *Princely India; Photographs by Raja Deen Dayal.* New York, 1980.

———, and Ainslie Embree. *The Last Empire: Photography in British India, 1855–1911.* Millerton, N.Y., 1976.

LITERATURE

Ali, Ahmed, ed. and trans. *The Golden Tradition: An Anthology of Urdu Poetry.* New York and London, 1973.

Forster, E. M. *The Hill of Devi.* New York, 1953.

Ingalls, Daniel H. *Sanskrit Poetry from Vidyakara's "Treasury."* Cambridge, Mass., 1979.

Jhabvala, Ruth Prawer. *Heat and Dust.* New York, 1977.

Mascaro, Juan, trans. *The Bhagavad Gita.* London, 1962.

Mehta, Rama. *Inside the Haveli.* New Delhi, 1977.

Merwin, W. S., and J. Masson Moussaieff. *The Peacock's Egg; Love Poems from Ancient India.* San Francisco, 1981.

Russell, Ralph, and Khurshidul Islam. *Ghalib Life and Letters.* Cambridge, Mass., 1969.

———. *Three Mughal Poets: Mir, Sauda, Mir Hasan.* Cambridge, Mass., 1968.

Ruswa, Mirza, Khushwant Singh, and M. A. Hosaini, eds. *The Courtesan of Lucknow.* Delhi, 1961.

Vatsyayana. *Kama Sutra of Vatsyayana.* Translated by Sir Richard Burton. New York, 1964.

WORKS RELATING TO INDIAN COSTUME AND TEXTILES

Alkazi, Roshen. *Ancient Indian Costume.* New Delhi, 1983.

Bean, Susan S. *Costumes from India in the Collection of the Costume Institute of the Metropolitan Museum of Art.* New York, 1982. Unpublished thesis.

Chandra, Moti. *Costumes, Textiles, Cosmetics, and Coiffure in Ancient and Medieval India.* New Delhi, 1973.

Chaudhuri, Nirad. *Culture in the Vanity Bag.* Bombay, 1976.

Dar, S. N. *Costumes of India and Pakistan.* Bombay, 1969; reprint 1982.

Fabri, Charles. *Indian Dress.* New Delhi, 1977.

Ghurye, G. S. *Indian Costume.* Bombay, 1951.

Irwin, John, and Margaret Hall. *Indian Painted and Printed Fabrics.* Ahmadabad, India, 1971.

Pant, G. N. *Indian Arms and Armour,* Vol. III, S. Attar Singh. New Delhi, 1983.

Platts, John T. *A Dictionary of Urdu, Classical Hindi and English.* Oxford, 1930.

Sharar, Abul Halim. *Lucknow: The Last Phase of an Oriental Culture.* Translated by E. S. Harcourt and Fakhir Hussain. London, 1975.

Singh, Chandramani. *Textiles and Costumes from the Maharaja Sawai Man Singh II Museum.* Jaipur, 1979.

Singh, Martand. *The Master Weavers.* Delhi, 1982.

Verma, Som Prakash. *Art and Material Culture in the Paintings of Akbar's Court.* New Delhi, 1978.

PHOTO CREDITS